Inside Australian Culture

Inside Australian Culture

Legacies of Enlightenment Values

Baden Offord, Erika Kerruish,
Rob Garbutt, Adele Wessell and Kirsten Pavlovic

Foreword by Ashis Nandy
Afterword by Vinay Lal

ANTHEM PRESS
LONDON · NEW YORK · DELHI

Anthem Press
An imprint of Wimbledon Publishing Company
www.anthempress.com

This edition first published in UK and USA 2015
by ANTHEM PRESS
75–76 Blackfriars Road, London SE1 8HA, UK
or PO Box 9779, London SW19 7ZG, UK
and
244 Madison Ave #116, New York, NY 10016, USA

First published in hardback by Anthem Press in 2014

British Library Cataloguing-in-Publication Data
A catalogue record for this book is available from the British Library.

Library of Congress Cataloging-in-Publication Data
The Library of Congress has cataloged the hardcover edition as follows:
Offord, Baden, 1958–
Inside Australian culture : legacies of enlightenment values / Baden Offord, Erika
Kerruish Rob Garbutt, Kirsten Pavlovic and Adele Wessell ;
Foreword by Ashis Nandy ; Afterword by Vinay Lal.
pages cm. – (Anthem Australian humanities research series)
Includes bibliographical references and index.
ISBN 978-1-78308-231-5 (hardcover : alk. paper)
1. Australia–Civilization. 2. Social values–Australia. 3. Cultural pluralism–Australia.
4. National characteristics, Australian. 5. Australia–Civilization–English influences. I.
Kerruish, Erika. II. Garbutt, Rob, 1961– III. Pavlovic, Kirsten.
IV. Wessell, Adele. V. Title.
DU107.O36 2014
994–dc23
2014016247
9781783084319

ISBN-13: 978 1 78308 431 9 (Pbk)
ISBN-10: 1 78308 431 6 (Pbk)

Cover image © Rob Garbutt

This title is also available as an ebook.

CONTENTS

Foreword

IS AUSTRALIA A VICTIM OF THE ETHICAL LIMITS OF THE ENLIGHTENMENT? A MODEST FOREWORD FOR AN IMMODEST VENTURE

Ashis Nandy

For more than two hundred years, the Enlightenment vision and the values it sanctions have provided the standard by which all cultures have been judged in the civilised world. It has shaped virtually every new imagination of a desirable society and every radical intervention in societies and states, even when – during this same period – Enlightenment values have also often been used to justify some of the major projects of Satanism in our times.

Everyone has the right to one's own clichés, as C. P. Snow used to say, so I reaffirm my belief that human beings, given enough time, opportunity and a culture of impunity, can turn any theory of salvation – secular or nonsecular – into its opposite. For instance, not only did the participants in the Atlantic slave trade find support in the idea of infrahuman Africans being brought into civilisation, but some who penned the world's first democratic constitution did not find it abnormal that they themselves had large, private retinues of slaves. Nor did the colonial powers in Asia and Africa hesitate to borrow from newly fashionable theories of evolution to justify their colonial conquests and to look at the colonised as newfound apprentices who would, in the long run, 'Europeanise' the globe. I, for one, find it impossible to trace the ethical, intellectual and political trajectory of the nineteenth century and the first half of the twentieth century without referring to the Enlightenment and the age of reason.

The two World Wars finally broke the spell. The use of nineteenth-century biology and eugenics, particularly the idea of natural 'selection' and the principle of 'the right to destroy life unworthy of life', were so blatant and thorough in Germany – Robert J. Lifton points out that these ideas were there since the 1920s, and did not emerge fully formed until the Third Reich – that even in Europe and North America there are now murmurs that earlier popular explanations of the barbarism of Third Reich as a betrayal of the Enlightenment cannot perhaps be taken as the full story. The simple-minded works of the likes of Erich Fromm, which saw Nazism as a pathological expression of an irrational fear of freedom and modernity, have given way to a more nuanced reexamination of the European heritage itself. After all, as early as the first decade of the twentieth century – when the Enlightenment values were well in place – the genocide of the Hereros and the Namas had already occurred, the concentration camp had been 'invented' and deployed by the British in South Africa, and famine had already been used as an instrument of state policy in Ireland. Among the later works on Nazi Germany, there has been, firstly, a vague, hesitant recognition, and then a more self-confident diagnosis of the role that was played by what I can only call pathologies of scientific rationality and perhaps of reason itself. That is the story of the European Holocaust as told by a whole series of scholars, from Hannah Arendt to Zygmunt Bauman.

Not that there were no earlier critics of the Enlightenment, modernity and Baconian science. William Blake (1757–1827), John Ruskin (1819–1900), Leo Tolstoy (1828–1910), Mohandas Gandhi (1869–1948) and Ananda Coomaraswamy (1877–1947) are obvious, if random, examples. But they were mostly seen as romantic traditionalists, transcendentalists and mystics, driven by uncompromising pastoralist visions and a visceral hatred of modernity and its urban–industrial commitment. And probably all of them except Gandhi, who was 'nasty' and cussed enough to 'enter the slum of politics', could be shelved as lovable instances of literary or ethical excess, not fit to comment upon the dirty world of politics and statecraft. Criticisms of modernity and challenges to values of the Enlightenment acquired a political edge when voices from the South, such as Gandhi and Rabindranath Tagore, began to hint at the complicity of Enlightenment values in cases of genocide and dehumanised exploitation, which had been customised for the lesser mortals in the tropics.

***

One would have thought that these arguments would make sense in Australia, a colonised society that was also a penal colony comprising not merely criminals exported from industrialising England, but also dissenters of diverse background – Irish anti-imperialists and freedom fighters, Luddites, others who were on the wrong side of the Enclosure movement, and Scottish and Welsh nationalists.

Early Australians knew that their country was designed to host not merely pioneers trying to harness nature – the unknown flora and fauna of Australia that included a whole range of Indigenous communities, but also those among the white immigrants who, according to officialdom, needed ideological discipline. This was to be done, if not through thought policing of the kind sometimes tried out in the case of the Aborigines, then at least through 'proper' education and socialisation. Such education and socialisation were double-edged tools. They ensured that Australia would never see itself as a once-colonised society, the way large parts of Asia and Africa do, and that there would always be a subterranean stream in Australian culture that would continue to see the country as a colonial, European power – a subaltern colonial power perhaps, but a colonial power nonetheless. This explains many of the anomalies in its official worldview, its ambivalent perceptions of its geographically close but psychologically distant neighbours, and its distinctive style of self-negotiation.

That discipline is now breaking down, and this book is another testimony to that. Years ago, I came across psychoanalyst Edmund Glover's formulation that even a wrong interpretation by a therapist has its uses. Presumably, learning to look within and acquiring the capacity to live with uncomfortable, even distressing interpretations of oneself can itself be a learning experience and a therapeutic intervention. I believe that even those who disagree with the main thesis of this book will also gain much from the effort. I certainly have.

During the last few years, I have read a number of self-exploratory works on Australia. They differ radically in their approach and conclusions, and cannot all be correct simultaneously. But even if most of them are flawed empirically and even politically, I like to believe that they are different parts of the same story. They are all products of a new awareness that is moving from the periphery towards the centre in that lonely continent. Obviously, something is happening there that cannot be easily reconciled with the global stereotype of Australia as an easygoing, sports-loving, beer-swilling, successful and developed welfare society. There are cracks in the mirror in which Australians used to see themselves.

Other countries have gone through similar phases of self-examination. Post–World War II Germany and its anguished self-negotiation is an obvious example, and the long, often-strident debate on India's self-definition is a crucial part of its political culture. In the United States, another immigrant society, such attempts to look within have had a mixed reception. They usually have come in clusters and, once the fashion has ebbed, proceed into glorious near-obscurity. The Americans have the gift of containing all dissent within small intellectual ghettos and sealing it off from the rest of the society, particularly from its mainstream media and its policy elite. Dissent flourishes in the United States as popular courses in famous universities and as respected cults that are politically irrelevant but are crucial components in the self-definition of the American elite and of the society's ethical ballast. They are 'rediscovered' for the general public on special occasions, and then the mainstream returns to its commitment to the time-tested algorithm of life. Will Australia's self-examination go the same way?

I doubt it. Australia is a small country that does not have much scope for containing dissent within pockets of sanitised, fashionable, academic islands as self-contained intellectual communities. The country's intellectual landscape seems, to me, close to being a face-to-face one that spills over the boundaries of universities, newspaper columns and party lines, and, ultimately, even begins to divide families. The public culture seems to me, an outsider, to be closer to that of South Africa than to that of 'the mother country', as some Australians may like to call England. I am inclined to believe that the number of books that have come out on the underside of Australia's self-definition and the darker side of its past – during the colonial period and, later, during the years it pursued the White Australia Policy – are a more radical intervention into the myth of origin with which every country lives and on which its culture of state is built.

This self-negotiation, however, is built on a mixture of denial and pained recognition of changing realities. For nearly two centuries, Australia was officially a phalanx of Europe in the Asia-Pacific region, not only geopolitically but also culturally. Indeed, in the high noon of colonialism, there seemed to be some cultivated forgetfulness in the country's policy elite that it was a colonised society. They looked at themselves as the junior partners of those who colonised, and aspired to one day be equal participants in the venture. Of course, there were dissenters who did not fit into this frame. In recent years, I have read about some of them and have come to admire their lonely, often doomed battles. But, as I have already proposed, mainstream Australia did not feel it was colonised in the way, say, the Irish felt they were. Australians considered themselves soldiers of the empire – foot soldiers undoubtedly, but soldiers nonetheless.

Strangely, it is this past that the country has begun to fight today with an apparatus that, in its case, is mostly inherited from the Enlightenment. Perhaps the Enlightenment also had as its underside strands of thought that could not be entirely wiped out by the triumphal march of what could be called unalloyed, uncompromising reason. There is, thus, a built-in double bind in this self-excavation.

If I can hazard a guess as to one of the sources of discomfort with the Enlightenment in the savage world for the sake of the authors of this book,

I shall say the following: a system of values that unconditionally prioritises reason cannot ultimately serve the purposes of any civilised society. Such values also have to be backed by compassion and empathy, however Victorian and Puritanical this may sound. When Offord, Kerruish, Garbutt, Pavlovic and Wessell discuss the limitations of the Enlightenment vision through three real-life problems that have at different times stumped public policy in Australia, it becomes more obvious that those who have questioned the official line – from the academy, media, judiciary and politics, including the authors of this volume – have mostly done so from outside the conventions of mainstream intellectual debate, whether they admit it or not. This has not impoverished Australia's political culture or maimed the intellectual exercise undertaken in the following pages, but has instead enriched and deepened them.

PREFACE AND ACKNOWLEDGEMENTS

The idea for this book came about while Professor Vin D'Cruz was Adjunct Professor in Alternative Future Studies in the School of Arts and Social Sciences at Southern Cross University between 2006 and 2008. The most inspiring and collegial of scholars, D'Cruz, with his usual acuity and enabling tactics, assembled a team of us in the School to collaborate and write a book on the urgent challenge of how Australian society would meet its future in an honest, frank and critically reflective way. He saw this book as part of a series of important scholarly works that summed up his most germane concerns, which cohered around the way in which Australia, as a multicultural society in Oceania, would come to terms culturally and intellectually with its proximity and future in Asia, and secondly, how it would ultimately engage substantively with the presence of the indigenous heart and mind belonging to the world's longest living civilisation.

As an innovative and illuminating way to respond to these concerns, D'Cruz looked to the ideas of Ashis Nandy, 'one of the foremost critical intellectuals on the globe',[1] as Raewyn Connell has noted. Nandy would be used as a lens through which to help us get inside Australian culture, so to speak. Testament to his energy, commitment and tenacity, D'Cruz did in fact manage to publish two books that tackled these concerns before he died in 2008. The first, *As Others See Us: The Australian Values Debate*,[2] was a postcolonial investigation of the politics and cultural issues surrounding a decade and more debate about the nature of what counted as Australian values. The book responded eloquently, critically and passionately to a range of pressing issues such as the Australian public cultural response to asylum seekers, dislocation from the environment and the hypocritical rhetoric behind social cohesion policies in the early part of the twenty-first century. The second collection, *Profiles in Courage: Political Actors and Ideas in Contemporary Asia*,[3] provided a powerful addition to the growing intellectual exchange between Australian and Asian intellectuals. It featured the ideas and lives of 17 leading Asian thinkers and activists (for example including Ashis Nandy, Akram Osman, Aung San Suu Kyi and Muhammad Yunis), exposing their contributions on culture, politics, sociology, history and economics to an Australian public. This book clearly demonstrated that national values are culturally contingent and always contested, structured in societies through institutions and the public sphere in a range of complex ways. What is important about both these volumes is that they underscore a new dimension in thinking about Australia and its place in the world. The seminal work of Raewyn Connell's *Southern Theory*, published in 2007,[4] had been for D'Cruz an important indicator and moment in the validation of a profound intellectual shift in Australian academic work towards the recognition of ways of knowing other than those offered by dominant European Enlightenment traditions.

Our work in this current book builds on D'Cruz's final two volumes noted above.[5] Together with his classic postcolonial analysis *Australia's Ambivalence towards Asia* (cowritten with William Steele)[6] these all contribute to a considerable *ouvre* that D'Cruz produced over more than half a century as an Australian-Asian scholar. The development of his thought, investigations and analyses can be viewed as an intellectual and ethical mirror of the radical changes that took place in Australian history over the last fifty years. He observed Australia struggling from a monocultural society into a multicultural reality, where its context was finally being recognised as both inherently connected to indigenous ontology and epistemology, positioned in the Asia-Pacific region of the world.

D'Cruz cared deeply and passionately about the future of Australia. Throughout the development of *Inside Australian Culture* he implored us to consider the possibility of Australia becoming an exemplar of overlapping cultures characterised by a robust cosmopolitan ethos. To illustrate this, D'Cruz drew our attention to Maria Rosa Menocal's book *Ornament of the World*,[7] which describes a precedent, a period in Spain's history where in Andalusia, southern Medieval Spain, for several hundred years Muslims, Christians and Jews lived and worked together to form a remarkable and resilient culture of tolerance. The compelling challenge that a multicultural society like Australia faces, D'Cruz argued, is whether it has the courage to wrestle with and resolve its own flagrant contradictions, not through violence or collective intellectual amnesia, but through shared knowing and by respectful cultural encounter. For D'Cruz, an Australian public culture capable of living with its own contradictions would be the hallmark of a mature society.

As the authors of this book, we come from a range of disciplinary backgrounds, which D'Cruz saw as a valuable strength. Between the five of us, we work across Australian studies, Asian studies, history, law, cultural studies and postcolonial studies, an expression perhaps of how scholarship in the field of Australian studies itself may be characterised as multidisciplinary and cross-disciplinary; but where Australia is the intellectual focus. Of course, a perceived weakness of our collective authorship is that the narrative flow may not always be as cohesive as it might be. In our own way we have attempted to honour D'Cruz, making the book as coherent as possible, but any deficiency in argument and structure of thought ultimately lies with us. It is our sincere hope that the book not only pays tribute to D'Cruz's legacy as a remarkable cultural thinker and analyst, but that it contributes to the field of Australian Postcolonial Studies in the way that D'Cruz intended.

This work, therefore, is the distillation of much effort and the results of a great deal of generosity over a number of years. We especially thank Professor Ashis Nandy of the Centre for the Study of Developing Societies who was kind enough to host several of us, including Vin D'Cruz, in December 2007 in Delhi where we conducted several days of interviews and discussions with him mulling over Australian culture. The rich dialogue and critical engagement with Nandy during this visit became the basis for the analytics, arguments and scope of this book. The visit was partly funded by a research grant from Southern Cross University. Baden Offord would also like to particularly thank Ashis Nandy for hosting him at the Indian International Centre in 2009, 2010 and 2012 as the project developed.

Part of D'Cruz's legacy was that he was an exemplary enabling scholar. Introducing us to the work of Ashis Nandy and then giving us the opportunity to spend time with one of India's most important social and cultural critical thinkers and theorists was a gift of connective scholarship. As the reader will see, Nandy plays a central role in the theorisation underpinning this book, similar to the other two volumes mentioned above. We are extremely grateful to Ashis Nandy agreeing to provide a foreword. We are also very honoured to have an afterword provided by the distinguished Indian scholar and historian Professor Vinay Lal (UCLA), which bookends the tricky intellectual efforts that we have organised here. Nandy and Lal are two of the most significant and important Southern theorists and postcolonial critics in the world today. They have generously given some polish to our project while shaking it up.

We would like to acknowledge the Centre for Peace and Social Justice at Southern Cross University for providing the intellectual space for many of the conversations that nourished this book and which hosted many of the research meetings that incubated our thinking. Also, we would like to thank Dr Susan Ballyn, director of the Centre for Australian Studies at the University of Barcelona, for providing a forum on a number of occasions where many of the ideas in this book were rehearsed. Thanks to Jennifer Nielsen, John Ryan and Christopher Macfarlane for editorial advice, and to Gerard Goggin for his suggestion to publish in the Anthem Australian Humanities Research Series. Thank you to the editors Rob Reddick, Brian Stone and Miranda Kitchener at Anthem for helping to considerably enhance the quality of the book and for bringing it to fruition, and to the anonymous reviewers who provided astute insights and critique, which we believe has made this a much better book, one that Vin D'Cruz would be happy with.

Baden Offord, Erika Kerruish, Rob Garbutt,
Adele Wessell and Kirsten Pavlovic

Chapter One

INTRODUCTION

Overview

This book focuses on three discrete historical moments in Australia's past read through the lens of Ashis Nandy, an Indian sociopolitical theorist, psychologist and contemporary cultural critic. This is not a historical enquiry as such, but rather a discussion to enable a critical and reflective line of thinking about how contemporary Australian public culture has been informed by an ongoing set of values and principles that come from its European Enlightenment legacy. We wish to draw attention to the limits of this legacy in order to help create a more just, equitable and reflective society where values and principles are drawn from all of its citizens.

Within a national context, values are never free floating. They are institutionalised, legitimated and expressed through the core institutions of a society, which include such important 'truth' makers such as the media, church, law and education. This serves a process of self-definition. As Edward Said has said:

> Self-definition is one of the activities practised by all cultures: it has a rhetoric, a set of occasions, and authorities (national feasts, for example, times of crisis, founding fathers, basic texts and so on), and a familiarity all its own.[1]

Values are thus normalised through ritual, story, politics and tradition. A nation comes to know itself through its values, and this produces the normative template for national knowing. Schooling and education, for example, though often very different projects, are both crucial domains in which values become respectively embedded and reproduced or examined and redefined. In Australia, the values which have become ubiquitous to its national story, and which underpin its institutions, have been formulated through efforts that are distinctive to a settler society, specifically to an Anglo-Celtic settler society with a British heritage. The values that have come to dominate society in Australia are linked to a chain of belonging and intellectual effort that has been inculcated and sustained through the British Enlightenment. European culture has been nurtured in the great southern continent in deliberative ways. For example, Anzac Day in Australia is a key national, ritualised event that is celebrated each year on the 25th of April. Originating from a battle fought (and lost) in the First World War at Gallipoli in Turkey in support of the British Empire, this tradition, which celebrates its centenary in 2015, has become a key site of Australia's civilising *modus operandi*. 'Its legend is etched deep in the nation's psyche', as Mick Dodson has put it.[2] Historically, Anzac is identified with the motif 'Lest We Forget', sustaining not just the commemoration of Gallipoli, but of all wars and battles that Australians have participated in. Anzac is regarded as foundational to many of the dominant values found in contemporary Australia. Every statue and memorial across Australia dedicated to Anzac is a site of national self-definition, a cultural, political and social marker that has mythologised a specific narrative of memory.[3] This sits alongside the fact that Australia remains a constitutional monarchy with Queen Elizabeth II as the formal head of state.

The argument of this book is based upon three key considerations. First, it seeks to contribute to academic work that interrogates the Australian nation as it has been imagined through the lens of the European Enlightenment legacy, investigating three moments that illustrate the formation of the imagined Australian community. Our purpose, however, is not to rehearse the Enlightenment's manifestation in Australia in enormous depth, as that has been more than satisfactorily accomplished by the historian John Gascoigne. Rather, we make a gesture to the salient architecture that characterises this legacy as it has impacted upon the formation and sustaining of Australian public culture.

Second, we regard the Enlightenment legacy within a colonial frame that has been installed through the mechanism of a settler society. In this book, we actively respond to the mindset that was created through colonialism in the Australian context. We see colonialism as an ongoing project in Australian public culture, one that has not yet been fully exposed or resolved partly due to the very limits of possible critique that can come from within the Enlightenment legacy. Thus, we cannot see how the very same colonised mind (and its institutional nodes) can decolonise itself. This is both the dilemma and the challenge. In this sense, we fully agree with Ashis Nandy's assessment that 'This colonialism colonises the mind in addition to bodies and it releases forces within colonised societies to alter their cultural priorities once and for all.'[4] In relation to Australia, cultural priorities that persist rest on a deep fear of the other within (the indigenous) and the other without (generic Asia, the migrant, asylum seeker).

Third, this book is a tool for thinking about how European Enlightenment values are installed and reified through mechanisms of public culture. As the

Australian composer Peter Sculthorpe once noted,[5] in the nineteenth century, more than 600,000 pianos were brought to Australia from across the seas, over the beaches, into ports and into cities, towns and farms, to actively enculturate the developing Australian public culture. This installation of European music into the emerging nation provides a powerful example of how values and ways of knowing become domesticated. Tony Hughes-d'Aeth in his essay, 'A Prospect of Future Regularity: Spatial Technologies in Colonial Australia', gives an indication of how the British mind would install its worldview. He quotes from Phillip's settlement journal: 'There are few things more pleasing than the contemplation of order and useful arrangement [...] this satisfaction cannot anywhere be more fully enjoyed than where a settlement of civilised people is fixing itself on a savage coast.'[6] In our book, we examine other kinds of ordering, where Enlightenment values are disclosed through contests and fault lines within the public culture. These contests are the specific effects of a public space in tension.

As Others See Us

As we flagged earlier, this book arose out of a suggestion by the late Professor J. V. D'Cruz. What might we find, he asked, if we looked at the way in which the British public culture that took hold in Australia after colonisation shaped its capacity to deal with racial and cultural difference? Examining some disparate moments in the formation of Australian public culture and showing how they demonstrate the struggle to respond to issues of cultural difference, could help us to better understand the Australian society of today. What, for example, are the terms of reference ubiquitous to Australia's public cultural engagement with difference? How have these terms of reference become the primary template upon which the majority of cultural, political and psychological expression in Australia has been framed? In undertaking such an adventurous analysis, why not, D'Cruz asked, also look to ideas developed in the examination of the political psychology of another country colonised by the British? This turn to an *other* theory might aid us in getting inside the dominant forms of Australian public culture by exercising a line of enquiry that moves away from the limitations prevailing in an analysis done from within that relies on using the usual suspects. The work of the Indian thinker, Ashis Nandy, is precisely useful in this regard.

D'Cruz's suggestions were fruitful, and Nandy's work proved useful for examining the hazards of Australian public culture for insiders and outsiders to British traditions. Enlightenment ideas took hold in an especially British form in Australia, making it difficult for those from non-British traditions to access Australia's public culture. This is partly because of the intimate relationship between Enlightenment ideas and other British traditions from which such ideas were not, and are not, always easily separated. These traditions include assumptions about the whiteness of the British and thus the Australian population, and the British foundations of Australian culture. While commentators might hope that the relationship between Australia's 'thick racial identity' and 'thin civic identity' might be broken, and multiculturalism embraced, this project is a complex and fraught one.[7]

As useful as the European Enlightenment tradition has been for fostering the public validation and evaluation of ideas in Australia, it pervasively restricted the terms according to which its public culture dealt with cultural and racial difference. All customs in some way establish such limits, but certain features of this specific tradition have rendered it particularly deaf to the worth of others as sound bases for values and standards. Two interrelated factors lie at the roots of this difficulty. Firstly, within the tradition, there is an inherent inability to acknowledge the value of diverse cultural traditions in general. Consequently, as a tradition, the Enlightenment has a special relationship to itself as such; or, more accurately, it is a way of knowing that does not acknowledge or value itself as a tradition. This means it is prevented from understanding itself as one tradition among others. Secondly, as we see so clearly in the three moments examined in this book – the 1858 inquiry into regulating Chinese immigration; the Cubillo v. the Commonwealth case of 2000; and the Cronulla Riot of 2005 – Enlightenment-derived public culture has demanded that different traditions justify and legitimate themselves through its own terms of reference. Few openings have been created to allow experiences, values and ideas originating outside of Enlightenment frames of thought to legitimately coexist with it.

These internal demands of Enlightenment traditions mean that they both resist seeing beyond themselves and, moreover, are hampered in articulating this problem (of seeing). While priding itself on the open debate of and challenge to received ideas, Enlightenment thinking nonetheless has not questioned certain of its own basic tenets, which we argue have developed into modern fundamentalisms. Therefore, it consequently inhibits or resists any recognition of its flaws, and undermines its accountability for acts perpetrated in its name. As a result, to put it simply, it is a tradition in need of assistance. In this respect, we have turned to Ashis Nandy to undertake a different way of theorising and understanding the dilemma of Enlightenment values in Australian public culture. This step towards other ways of knowing, in order to facilitate self-examination, is both compelling and necessary.

One way we can characterise the path we have taken in this examination of Australia's public culture is to describe it as, to use Raewyn Connell's terminology, an exploration of the limits of 'Northern theory' for articulating the dynamics of Australian public culture, and a turn to 'Southern theory' to address some of those gaps, blind spots and blurry shadows. Thus, the theoretical and lived tradition transplanted from Europe and installed in Australia struggles to adequately examine and renew itself, but can be assisted by the generosity of Southern social theory, in this case the work of Nandy. If Northern theory tries to 'theorise the formation of social institutions and systems from scratch, in a blank space', with our turn to the South we want to deploy theory that 'does not claim universality for a metropolitan point of view, does not read from only one direction, does not exclude the experience and social thought of most of humanity, and is not constructed on *terra nullius*.'[8] Our point in using Nandy's work is not to claim that his ideas apply universally to the experience of the colonised and the coloniser, but rather to look at how the continuities between India and Australia arising out of British colonisation can help us to think about Australia's difficulties in dealing with cultural difference in the past and particularly in the present.

The usefulness of such resources from India for our enterprise is a fine example of how productive it is to situate Australian culture not just in relationship to the Anglo and the non-Anglo, but amidst multiple relationships, such as those between the metropole and the periphery, the colonised and the coloniser, the West and the East, and the North and the South. Pursuing the complexity of the geographical, historical, cultural and economic relations amidst which Australia is located allows us 'to recognise […] that Australia, too, despite the fact that it now firmly considers itself "Western", is the outcome, not the original, of the Westernisation/modernisation of the world.'[9] This acknowledgement allows us to better articulate and analyse the dynamics of its cultures – its positives, negatives and ambivalences. Only when understanding Australian public culture as situated amidst this complexity are we able to usefully talk about the experiences of people like our colleague, J. V. D'Cruz. He was Catholic, born in British-occupied colonial Malaya to an Indian family, with an adopted Chinese brother. He experienced the Japanese invasion and occupation of Malaya, saw the British army retreat during World War II, experienced the Communist Party's (composed predominantly of ethnic Chinese) efforts to gain power in Malaya, lived in post-Gandhi India for seven years after 1958 and arrived in Australia in the mid-1950s. No simple division between East and West, North and South, or colonised and coloniser can engage with the cultural dynamics of his life, or that of many others.[10]

Situating an understanding of Australia's public culture in such a context can hopefully stimulate its curbed accountability. As Nandy points out, it is vital for traditions to reflect on themselves and answer for their actions if they are to renew themselves and flourish into the future. British culture, unified and hardened through the experience of colonialism, needs to be decolonised and diversified into its numerous traditions. Within Australia, as Henry Reynolds points out, historically there have been European humanitarian traditions advocating for the better treatment of Indigenous Australians, despite the prevailing climate working against this.[11] And John Gascoigne demonstrates that there was an array of British cultural traditions, religious and otherwise, at play in colonial Australia, although some were sidelined in the formation of its public culture.[12] Space for the continuation of these and other traditions needs to be secured. This requires the revisiting of past events, as these historians have done, in order to recover what has been suppressed and marginalised, and reintroduce it into the past, present and future. The need for alternative futures does not only apply to non-Anglo traditions attempting to avoid the prescriptions of a universal modernity, it also applies to the traditions arising from Anglo-British cultures.

The reemergence of questions of cultural difference and tradition in our examination of Australian public culture should not surprise us, for 'the rocks on which the fantasy of a globalised, universal modernity foundered were the actual, irreducible cultural differences which the modern project wished to eradicate but found itself unable to.'[13] The project of a universalising and totalising modernity gave way to a proliferation of 'indigenised modernities.' But this idea of multiple modernities needs to be qualified by pointing out that some of them are more closely aligned with modernity – as understood in the conventional sense – than others, and the implications of this for their access to power need to be closely considered.

One way of characterising some cultures unaligned with modernity – as understood in the conventional sense – is as 'little' or 'local cultures.' These little and local cultures are those, according to D'Cruz, that draw on 'forms of knowledge and living that do not look to the European Enlightenment or its modern progenies for their validation.'[14] Many such little cultures are under threat or are undervalued, often effaced by nationalist history and concerns. Recovering the value of culture in general is part of recognising their worth. Valuing little cultures and ensuring they flourish requires us to examine the dynamics between them, as well as those dynamics between little cultures and projects of colonisation, nationalism and modernity. Indeed, we think that the capacity to deal with little and local cultures can be considered a measure of a nation's openness to difference and the sophistication of its resources for engaging with them.

Australian public culture still struggles to adequately debate and discuss questions of racial and cultural difference, especially in terms of how to engage inclusively with residents and visitors from cultures that significantly differ from Anglo-Celtic ones. There seems to have been a turning away from the inflaming of racial anxiety and tension that occurred so visibly under the Howard government and which was marked by incidents such as the MS

Tampa[15] and the Cronulla Riot (the focus of chapter six). But the difficulties of racial and cultural difference persist, and can be seen in the debate surrounding asylum-seeker arrivals in 2013, in which the usual, anxious narratives were all too ready to leap to the fore to guide and inform the public discussion. The MA Tampa incident in 2001 was quickly depicted as a looming crisis, a 'tidal wave' that threatened national security and health. There was public pressure for the government to toughen up and adopt a 'harder' stance so that Australia would not be flooded with 'boat people.'[16] Nonsensationalist discourses regarding asylum seekers – ideas like asylum-seeker numbers being linked to the conditions in their country of origin – were not readily taken up. The resistance to such discourse is partly because racial and cultural hierarchies are ingrained in Australian public culture itself, hindering it from usefully responding to the dynamics of questions of racial and cultural difference. Our point in referring to this incident in which questions of race and culture are at stake is not to argue the details of all the relevant issues, but to show how Australian public culture retains limited resources for responding to incidents of racism and questions of racial and cultural difference.

  D'Cruz arrived in Australia as a student to face, on the one hand, the institutionalised racism of the White Australia Policy, and on the other a degree of tolerance toward people of colour. We can compare the experiences of today's overseas students with those of D'Cruz in the 1950s, who writes:

> The dominant Australian culture, equipped with the confidence bestowed by Allied victory, was thereby enabled to welcome overseas students with a great deal less anxiety, occasionally in the manner that one would welcome and pat bewildered creatures that had strayed in. Except for the period of the 6 o'clock 'swill', when Australians downed as many beers as they possibly could between 5 and 6pm, before the law and the publicans poured them onto the streets, where they snarled and abused people-of-colour if encountered. If they cornered us overseas students, they would claim to recognise us by our mothers' and aunts' features, which they announced they got to know very well, really well indeed.[17]

Here we see matters of confidence and anxiety in cultural tradition, tolerance and racism and responses to difference, in a configuration different from, but not discontinuous with, today's. The demise of the White Australia Policy and efforts to cultivate a multicultural society notwithstanding, Australian public culture still needs to develop its resources and vocabulary for responding to questions of racial and cultural difference, and incidents and allegations of racism.

  British Enlightenment culture can never be just another cultural strand in Australia; its place in the history of Australian colonisation and the establishment of its public institutions and practices precludes that. But it can regard its place differently and remain open to critical evaluation and change, questioning and amending its tenets, such as those relating to individualism, history and knowledge. As a tradition, it is not uniform, static or self-contained, but rather open to reinterpretation and renewal. A desirable result of renewal would be to move away from the tradition seeing itself as the adjudicator between cultures, the gatekeeper to a public culture based on its own values and standards. Instead it could reconstruct itself as one of multiple public cultures, part of a public landscape that successfully engages with a variety of little, local and other traditions, and that recognises the practices of critical reflection within them.

Towards a Reflective Culture

Australia presents itself as a liberal democratic nation whose values are derived from Judeo-Christian and European intellectual traditions. It sees itself as part of Western civilization, and as such has defined its past, present and future based on this key assumption through the shaping of its modernity. Australia's self-definition and imagination has been constructed through a process of othering, as we argued earlier, that has been systemic and pervasive in its core institutions. This is the Australia that, in relation to asylum seekers and refugees, cries 'send the boats back', demonises them and redacts them from people to 'illegals.' Australia sees itself as a humanitarian, tolerant and hospitable society in the Western tradition, but at the same time, it is also an anxious nation,[18] based on a deep and profound unease with its geographical context, the reality of Indigenous presence and its multicultural everyday life.

The Australian story through modernity has been framed largely through heated debates about immigration, multiculturalism, refugees and asylum seekers, frequently through a focus on a monolithic Asia. What is now evident is an intensification of the interpenetration and overlapping of cultures and peoples in everyday life in Australia. As it has become a multicultural, multireligious and multiethnic reality – with a much keener sense of its Indigenous heart and mind – its public culture has become increasingly defined by intense conversations and inter-epistemic dialogue that are cosmopolitan and potentially decolonising. We believe that it will be through knowing Australia's Indigenous, Asia-Pacific and multicultural context that its values will be ultimately transformed. That is, it will happen through a process of self-knowing and therefore self-education based on a cosmopolitan ethic that understands that no one culture has a fix on truth. How this can be nurtured and sustained will be the challenge. It will demand new ways of conceiving what is required for Australia to go beyond its historical ambivalence towards Asia, its refusal to fully recognise and accept Aboriginal ontological belonging[19] and its multicultural reality. What we do know is that Australia, as an insular nation with flagrant contradictions (ideologically still meta-racially imagined as white, but experienced through colour, Indigenous recognition and cultural diversity), is being radically reoriented through the effects of its own self-understanding public culture, assisted by those from other traditions and ways of knowing.[20]

Moving towards a reflective culture therefore requires a cosmopolitan commitment (marked by inter-epistemic dialogue) as well as a decolonising intellectual framework. In respect to such an approach, Deborah Bird Rose has argued:

> The process of decolonising modern settler societies is a new phenomenon; we have no models from the past to guide us. It is equally a dialogical project; we cannot theorise in advance just how it will happen and still be committed to openness. We have to work it out step by step dialogically with and among each other.[21]

Crucial to this venture is engaging in rigorous, honest and robust conversation and dialogue about the nature of Australian culture, as we attempt to do in this book. This means digging into the past to understand how contemporary Australian identity and values have been formed. As Mick Dodson has eloquently remarked,

> When we can look at the past without flinching, when we can deal empathetically and more honestly with the searing parts of our history, then we can make real progress together. It would make our remembering complete. Without that honesty, the conversation hasn't even truly begun.[22]

Towards this end, a decolonising and cosmopolitan commitment aids such honest reflection and conversation. Soenke Biermann argues, 'We might understand decolonisation as the unravelling of assumed certainties and the re-imagining and re-negotiating of common futures.'[23] Essential to the nurturing of a cosmopolitan and decolonising perspective will be the need to develop intellectual strategies for getting inside Australian culture, understanding the dominant Enlightenment template and acknowledging its limitations. At the outset, a basic premise we work with is that Australia has not been decolonised. As the Lebanese-Australian anthropologist, Ghassan Hage, has commented:

> This is what constitutes the objective difficulty of the Australian situation. For a long time to come, Australia is destined to become an unfinished Western colonial project as well as a land in a permanent state of decolonisation.[24]

Structure and Style of the Book

Getting inside Australian culture is a difficult intellectual undertaking and not always easy. Given the enormous complexity of how values have been installed through institutional processes and the narratives of belonging that have developed within Australian public culture around issues such as race and migration, the investigation becomes an ethically charged endeavour that requires multiple views and voices. How can Australian culture become more conscious of itself, of the contradictions inherent in a system of values that essentially derive from an ongoing colonial process that is epistemologically constrained and limited? What are the intellectual tools available that can assist us in responding to this question? *Inside Australian Culture* is a response to these questions. As a book with a collective Australian authorship in dialogue and conversation with the Indian scholars Ashis Nandy and Vinay Lal, who are both from outside Australia, we deliberately create a form of Australian scholarship that is explicitly engaged with outside thinking. We are following in the Bakhtin tradition 'that it is not enough to simply understand the other's perspective. Only if it is made other than itself by being seen from outside can it produce something new or enriching.'[25] By creating an enquiry that is multiauthored and bookended by being seen from the outside, we make the point that such scholarship can produce a robust and nuanced contribution to contemporary debates about Australia's ongoing self-definition. Our aim is to test specific ideas and moments in relation to what has informed and continues to nourish Australian public culture.

The book is organised in three parts. In the first part we outline background conceptual considerations of what is required to get inside Australian culture. We sketch how Enlightenment ideas are central to the prominent debates and projects of colonial, settler Australia, setting its terms as a modern nation. We then make a survey of the content of Australian civil society through a discussion of its public culture and sphere, identifying predominant themes and issues through which these terms reverberate.

In the second part of the book we provide three chapters that investigate three moments in the past – the 1858 inquiry into regulating Chinese immigration; the *Cubillo v. the Commonwealth* case of 2000; and the Cronulla Riot of 2005. These events are selected because they illustrate how Enlightenment ideas echo through three, very different, key sites of public culture, fixing limits and contradictions for debates concerning cultural and racial difference. These case studies can be read as discrete chapters in themselves.

In the final part of the book we provide a Southern theoretical intervention by turning to the work of Ashis Nandy to assist us in getting inside Australian culture in a nuanced and reflective manner. We follow the Australian author

David Malouf's sage injunction that, 'We must rub our eyes and look again, clear our minds of what we are looking for to see what is there.'[26] In doing so, we are not assuming that in order to properly be conscious of the limits of Enlightenment ideas we need only the intellectual acuity of Nandy. But we suggest, following D'Cruz, that the endeavour of Australia becoming a reflective culture requires many explorations and stories, and Nandy's important place in postcolonial and cultural theory is undeniable. We see his insights as having a special clarity, and for this reason the reader will note that we have integrated Nandy's observations about Australian culture and the legacy of the European Enlightenment at the beginning of each chapter. These short but insightful comments by Nandy are presented as springboards into the following discussions, case studies and concluding remarks.

Part One

GETTING INSIDE AUSTRALIAN PUBLIC CULTURE

Chapter Two

THE ENLIGHTENMENT
AND TRADITION IN EARLY
COLONIAL SOCIETY

The Enlightenment vision also is a very, over the last two-and-a-half centuries, totalising posture because it thinks it is the last word in human history. It's as if Europe in the eighteenth century found the final answers to certain kinds of specific problems of human public life – and all that we can do now is to make minor editorial changes.

Interview with Ashis Nandy, 6 December 2007

In Australia, as in many other parts of the world, ideas and practices that have come to be termed the Enlightenment shepherded in modernity and installed measures of value, frameworks for social decision making and yardsticks for public debate. The subject of our discussion below is the way in which Enlightenment ideas, often those from the British Enlightenment, came to form the terms and values of early New South Wales' (NSW) public culture and social order, favouring some traditions while marginalising and suppressing others.

Enlightenment thought took shape in relationship to the traditions present in the colony, despite the difficulty much Enlightenment thought had in acknowledging other traditions as a condition of understanding and as valuable in their own right. The specific circumstances of Australian colonisation and the presence of both supporting and resistant traditions meant that the mainly British Enlightenment ideas in Australia took on specific characteristics. As John Gascoigne writes in *The Enlightenment and the Origins of European Australia*, an account on which this discussion relies, 'the set of ideas which the term "the Enlightenment" describes was capable of taking different forms in different situations [...] And in Australia, as elsewhere, local circumstances meant that some aspects of Enlightenment ideology received greater emphasis than others.'[1] The configuration of religious, political, educational and other traditions in the colony determined the ways in which ideas took, or did not take, hold. While Enlightenment thinking is often thought to view traditions as irrational superstitions associated with more primitive ways of life, as obstacles to knowledge and social progress, we argue that in practice the deployment of Enlightenment ideas in the colony was impossible without preexisting traditions by which they were shaped and with which they were enmeshed.

Born Modern: Securing an Enlightenment Social Order

To speak of a single Enlightenment, as Pocock and others point out, is misguided.[2] There were a variety of different Enlightenments that changed with national, social and political contexts, as well as the predilections of individual thinkers. Nevertheless, the time period roughly co-extensive with the eighteenth century was the setting for these instances of Enlightenment in Europe, in which were laid the intellectual foundations for modernity in its emphasis on liberty, rationality and open public debate. During this era, the belief burgeoned that universal principles governing nature, humanity and society could be discovered through the application of this understanding and approach. In turn, these principles were seen to furnish the basis for revising knowledge, human practices and social orders along truer, more effective and just lines. Universal principles and their practice demanded the challenging of customs and traditional authorities, and their rational justification.

Despite the difficulty in formulating a single Enlightenment project across its different instances (and sociohistorical contexts), John Robertson points out that its most unifying notion is that of material human betterment through the application of understanding, and he discusses three main aspects of this Enlightenment notion.[3] Firstly, he notes a common concern with the examination of the nature and behaviour of individuals through science, and the location of the individual in the context of human society rather than divine authority. Secondly, Enlightenment thinkers maintained the idea that material betterment and political economy are to be investigated for the sake of human progress. Finally, he observes a shared concern with what civilisation is and how it evolved. Although not all Enlightenment thinkers subscribed to the doctrine of progress or were optimistic about human nature (for example, David Hume subscribed to a decidedly gloomy view of humanity's future), the idea of progress was inherent in the notion that a universal, scientific rationality could be applied to society, improve its practices, challenge its traditions and correctly evaluate civilisations and cultures. These three core concerns are all apparent in Enlightenment traditions that were influential in the early years of European colonisation of Australia.

In its plans to improve both the land and its people, European settler society enthusiastically adopted the understanding of betterment as the idea that humans are sure to improve their condition through the application of scientific method. The English and Scottish Enlightenment thought that influenced the young Australian colony stressed the importance of progress, and the drive for progress was no mere theoretical matter. No doubt due to the precarious early years of the colony, during which food was in short supply, progress took a particularly tangible form and Gascoigne observes that 'the ideal of improvement transmitted a belief in the possibilities of progress into the fabric of everyday life, making more than a speculative system of philosophy.'[4] The Australian continent was regarded as uncultivated, possibly barren and unproductive. The minds and morals of convicts 'were the kind of raw material which seemed to cry out for the order which humanitarianism offered,'[5] and Aborigines were perceived to be in dire need of European civilising customs. In England, 'improvement' was a label applied to land use, serving as a code for capitalist farming, and this meaning came to the fore in Australia.[6] Indeed, the idea of improvement was built into the very notion of land tenure that allowed British occupation and the dismissal of Indigenous rights over land. John Locke's idea, echoed in Emmerich de Vattel's writings on international law, that for something to be considered property it had to be taken from the state of nature and mixed with labour, saw improvement of the land through work as essential to property rights. Colonists argued that Indigenous Australians had not laboured on the land because there was no sign of European-style agricultural improvement, and thus they had no property rights over land.[7] James Cook, in an act that disobeyed instructions to only claim the land if it was uninhabited or if the natives gave their consent, claimed the land with this justification. Likewise, Adam Smith's notion that every property owner was obliged to cultivate and improve a certain portion of the land he owned was applied to the early land grants.[8]

For reasons of survival and profit, British colonists wanted to make the land productive according to their own needs and terms, to retrieve it from a seemingly untouched state of nature. Native vegetation was dismissed practically and epistemologically as a possible source of foodstuffs; the plants and animals brought from Britain, initially on the advice of Joseph Banks, were to remedy this situation and install 'correct' food. Enlightenment ideas were present in the chosen pairs of stock and seed for agricultural produce and were articulated in plans, instructions and pamphlets. The precarious origins of the settlement, perceived oddity of its environment, and the need to secure food supplies drove agricultural development and encouraged a pragmatic approach based on science. The production of scientific knowledge of the world via the classification and investigation of the natural world was guided by necessity rather than curiosity. Natural science acquired an empirical emphasis and a resistance to theory.[9] In this process, Indigenous rights, land use and knowledge were disregarded, and the superiority of European scientific method and knowledge asserted. The instrumentalism of science in early NSW extended to its role in justifying European dominance and occupation through the belief that a superior civilisation was marked by its apparent technological superiority.

The way in which Enlightenment understandings of man and society were adopted and implemented had a pragmatic emphasis, reflecting the specific material and psychological circumstances of early colonial society. This further accentuated the pragmatism already present in the British Enlightenment tradition, which was, according to Roy Porter, 'more than mere worldliness: it embodied a philosophy of expediency.'[10] The political culture of the colony was formed by liberalism as it emerged from British Enlightenment thinking and worked against the all-encompassing power of the early governors and others with hierarchical tendencies. In the effort to combat elitist and aristocratic forces in the colony, such as those of the 'shepherd kings', both utilitarian and rights theories were used to advocate the equality of man, despite tensions between utilitarianism's instrumentalism and theories of the rights of man. This use of incompatible theories to combat the power of governors and pastoralists was a result of prioritising practical needs over theoretical cogency.

Locke's natural rights theory provided one basis on which a NSW government, and its limits, could be established. The thought of the late Enlightenment thinker and utilitarian, Jeremy Bentham, was also influential. His views about government and legislature, including his explicit writings about the political circumstances of the colony, provided another foundation for questioning the governor's powers and challenging the soundness of the NSW Constitution on the grounds that the powers of the executive and the legislature were not separate.[11] John Macarthur, engineer of the Rum Rebellion of 1808, was influenced by Bentham's as well as Locke's tradition of 'rightful rebellion against unlawful rule.'[12] Gradually, ideas such as the protection of liberty, equality before the law, freedom of the press, religious tolerance and the separation of church and state came to shape the public sphere and the political discourse. With Richard Bourke's Church Act of 1836, it was clear that there was to be no established church, with the Anglican, Scottish Presbyterian and Catholic churches to be equally funded by the state. After 30 years of settlement and the introduction of a small NSW council that was required to pass laws, the governor ceased to rule alone. By 1852, there were legislative assemblies in NSW, Victoria, Tasmania and South Australia, and plans for self-government.

Rights discourse in the colony was moderated by a practical emphasis on social utility, and the instrumental arm of Enlightenment thought steered colonial politics. The colony's emphasis on social utility and stability meant that political theories and practices based on the rights of man were often seen as threatening and in need of limitation within practical bounds. Thomas Paine's thought on rights and republican principles, with its more democratic emphasis, reached Australia but largely remained a limited, underground and subversive influence due to the colony's preference for judicious reform. The idea that man had inalienable rights was part of colonial political discourse, but in a precarious settlement amidst the atmosphere left by the French Revolution, ideas of rights were downplayed due to their potential threat to social stability, which the colony could ill afford.[13] Alan Atkinson notes that 'the French Revolution of 1789 was to disrupt and complicate the progress of enlightenment. It hurried the evolution of new ideas about civil order and the relationship between government and people, and in some minds, both revolutionary and counter-revolutionary, it sharpened an insistence that discipline should be met with silence.'[14] While a variety of British political dissidents were transported to the colony, they generally did not sustain their radical political interests.[15]

Shaping a society according to Enlightenment principles not only requires the reform of political institutions and a challenging of the governor's power, but it also requires the cultivation of its subjects. Education was a key means of promoting ideas such as human betterment. State intervention in education was considered particularly necessary in Australia, given its nature as a penal colony and an expected low rate of voluntary participation in education. Bentham's ideas were especially popular in Australian educational practices, even more so than in Britain, with their focus on categorisation and ordering students according to their progress. Underlying this view of human betterment through education was the belief that human nature was fundamentally of one kind and that differences were the result of varied influences and environments. Educational theory in general was based on the belief that the student's nature was essentially a clean slate that could be inscribed with whatever was desired. Christians and nonbelievers alike believed that education and the development of people's minds were the main means by which to improve humans. This common ground often overcame tension between the idea of human improvement and Christian original sin. Nevertheless, there was church opposition from both Catholics and Protestant dissenter traditions to the establishment of a secular education system. A central matter of debate was whether improvement of the intellect necessarily led to the improvement of morals, or whether separate religious instruction in morals was necessary. In the end, however, the impetus of the difficulty of maintaining multidenominational systems in sparsely settled areas and the absence of an established church meant that secular state education took hold in the colony even more vigorously than it did in the homeland of Britain.

Denominational religious instruction was deemed inessential to the improvement of the population.[16]

These struggles over the constitution of the education system were not just about what the best education is – secular or religious, state or church – they were highly political in terms of the debates of the time about social elitism. For instance, Bishop Broughton advocated a form of religious schooling with the goal that education should be appropriate to different social classes. Education, as a focussed battleground for the relationship between a secular state and traditional churches, was understood to be especially significant because it was seen to form the particular kinds of individuals that were required for the existence of a different kind of social order.

Of course, it was not only the British colonists who were thought to be in need of improvement in the early years of settlement. Social-contract theories, of both the Lockean and the Hobbesian variety, projected the myth of man in a state of nature onto the continent's Indigenous population. The Hobbesian approach considered the state of nature to be chaotic and violent, whereas the Lockean view thought it more neutral. However, both saw it as a state that had to be left behind for a civilised society to be attained. In the early years of Australian settlement, there was a widespread belief that the differences between the Indigenous population and the colonists were the result of culture and environment rather than intrinsic, biological differences. Stadial theory, particularly popular in Scottish brands of Enlightenment thought, saw Indigenous societies as the first in a number of stages of human development in a process of transition from barbarism to civilisation.[17] This theory saw all humanity as of one kind, only distinguished by levels of civilisation. The idea of an individual's life progress through childhood, development and then maturity was projected onto societies. This projection is explicit in Governor Phillip's declaration to Bennelong, 'I am the governor, your father.'[18] As a child's inevitable future was to grow to adulthood, Indigenous cultures' inevitable future was an Enlightenment social order in the form of British modernity.

Advocates of such a theory thought that if Indigenous people adopted a European lifestyle – participated in education and other 'civilising' processes – they could be schooled in the ways of a supposedly more advanced European society. Governor Macquarie, a product of the Scottish Enlightenment, asked Aborigines 'to relinquish the wandering idle and predatory Habits of Life, and to become industrious and useful Members of a Community where they will find Protection and Encouragement.'[19] He exercised his paternalism and created the 'native institution' to cater for the educational and health requirements of Aborigines. Like elsewhere in British colonies, Indigenous peoples were regarded as childlike and in need of guidance from a mature, rational (British) administrator.[20] There were very few colonists who did not support the idea that Indigenous people needed to abandon their nomadic life and cultivate crops. The idea that education and environment could shape individuals who would constitute the new and improved social order lay behind the ideas and practices of removing Indigenous children from their own people and educating them in a European fashion – practices that continued into the late twentieth century with the Stolen Generations.

The ready adoption of ideas of human betterment, science and education in colonial Australia reflects how the rupture of leaving Britain for Australia meant that some traditions were difficult to uphold in the new continent. Donald Horne writes that settler societies are in a sense 'born modern' because of this rupture with tradition.[21] The absence of an established church and other religious institutions assisted breaks from and a questioning of church traditions. Many British traditions (including Romanticism) did not map well on to the Australian landscape, encouraging a reliance on the principles of reason and understanding in their more pragmatic incarnations. The alien Australian landscape was felt to provide little support for the British imagination, including Romantic ideas of transcendence, so traditional practices and festivals were abandoned.[22] As Stephen Muecke writes, 'When the European modern gets transported to a place such as Australia it becomes dislocated from its sacred sites, disorienting the settlers.'[23] In this sense, tradition – thought of as the collective myths, beliefs and values that are part of a group's identity and that ensure continuity between the past, present and future – was disrupted for the British colonists. Deportation or immigration to Australia was an interruption to the traditions that carry across generations and that give a group a sense of identity and continuity over time.

The different environment and its demand for new practices not only interrupted tradition conceived of as continuity with the past; it also drove a break with tradition in the sense of a structure of knowledge. The inherited knowledge systems of the European colonists were simply not effective in the new continent's environments, which were so different to the British Isles. Gascoigne writes that, 'the Europeans were to learn the limitations of their new country which was not always amenable to techniques developed to deal with the fertile and well-watered land of Britain.'[24] The limited use of traditional forms of knowledge (especially regarding agriculture) fostered a reliance on scientific method as a source of knowledge for effective agricultural practices.

Enlightenment ideas took a particular form and hold in European colonial society in Australia, coming to be the dominant terms in its public culture. Science was believed to be able to solve the mysteries of the natural world, including coming to terms with the unfamiliar environment of the continent. It was also considered able to uncover the principles governing humans and human society, and thus render the convict colony a stable, modern society embarked on a process of betterment. The foundational myths that underpin modern industrial societies, such as beliefs in material progress and reality as economic and human betterment through the application of rationality, came to justify the Australian social order. Nevertheless, Enlightenment ideas – however abstract in aspiration – came in an embodied form, and their particular form in the colony was distilled in the context of a variety of traditions.

Support and Resistance: The Persistence of Tradition

Despite a loosening of the hold of tradition in colonial societies, we suggest that it was precisely the *survival* of some traditions that fostered the spread of Enlightenment ideas in the Australian colonial society. Practices that were justifiable by appeal to Enlightenment principles but too far from British customs remained unaccepted in public discourse. When it came to comparing women of the convict class to middle-class women, the liberal drive for equality never overcame the need to maintain an immense imaginative and conceptual distance between convict 'whores' and the graces of middle-class womanhood. The widespread homosexuality in the colony, no matter how justifiable both through rights and utilitarian theory, was repressed and unmentioned in the colony.[25]

Enlightenment ideas in early Australia, usually British ones, sat alongside some traditions and their practices more comfortably than others. In such instances, Enlightenment ideas mapped readily onto historically related traditions in a mutually supportive relationship and were readily adopted. Traditions that were radically different from the Enlightenment framework and did not share a similarity of ideas and values resisted its endeavours. Such traditions struggled for recognition and were sidelined in the public discourse of the colony. In this way, Enlightenment thinking effectively suppressed some traditions while cultivating and benefiting from others.

The idea that the Enlightenment could comfortably coexist with religious practices, given its tenet that critical rationality should be applied to all traditions, is initially counterintuitive. However, such coexistence is made understandable by appreciating that the Enlightenment's primary interest was and is to understand human progress rather than to eliminate religious belief and clericalism. Although it did not have a strong hold in Christianity prior to the Enlightenment, the idea of a 'future for mankind' is an Augustinian insight. Robertson writes that the Augustinian–Epicurean idea that 'men were weak and driven by their passions, to the extent that their pursuit of their own utility was scarcely compatible with the maintenance of society' and 'the conviction that the problem of unsociability could only be resolved in the course of history, in a process of socialisation' were foundations of Enlightenment thinking.[26] The individualism at the heart of the liberal ordering of social and political institutions was similarly derived from Christianity, with its emphasis on individual salvation. Although not political in nature, Christianity's universalism in its notion of the original equality of all souls can also be seen as continuous with ideas of equality and universalism that later emerge in political discourse.[27] In this way, ideas of progress, betterment and individualism resemble and resonate with forms of Christian tradition.

The Christian religious traditions that arrived with the early colonists played an important part in facilitating the adoption of Enlightenment thought in a variety of ways. British and local administrators considered religion to be conducive to cultivating social order and thus a potential ally in the project of improving the country's land and inhabitants. The early colony contained a mixture of religious practitioners, including Anglicans, Presbyterians, Protestant dissenting churches, Evangelicals and, increasingly, Catholics. This multiplicity of Christian traditions, rather than the clear dominance of one, helped to promote a secular state by discouraging an established church dominance and by supporting the separation of church and state. Along with the diversity of the Christian traditions present, many of the religious practices in the colony were of a variety that accepted many Enlightenment ideas. This continued an especially British approach to the relationship between reason and religion, in which, Porter writes, Enlightenment 'took place within, rather than against, Protestantism.'[28] The Scottish and Anglican churches brought with them the tradition of the coexistence of Christianity and Enlightenment ideas, and both broadly supported the idea that people could benefit from the exercise of reason. By stressing the way religion could profit from the application of reason, the established churches of England and Scotland had successfully removed 'the more threatening features of Enlightenment criticism of established institutions.'[29] In the nervous atmosphere of the French and American revolutions, this coexistence was politically useful because it allowed rulers to call on both Enlightenment principles and the authority of the divine in order to foster social stability.

Not all similarities between Christianity and Enlightenment thought were so easily called upon to maintain social stability. English liberalism was not associated so much with anticlericalism as with religious nonconformity.[30] The English doctrines of natural rights and radical Protestant interpretations of scripture both saw men born in equality with an innate right to freedom, and provided a basis from which to challenge the existing social order. This association is echoed in early NSW in the arguments of John Dunmore Lang, a Protestant Dissenter who argued against the pastoralist political hold by invoking 'the indefeasible rights of man.'[31]

This continuity between the Enlightenment and the Anglican and Scottish churches meant that, despite the establishment of a secular education system and the absence of an established church, the churches present in Australia were not necessarily on such an equal footing as it might initially seem. The Catholic church, to cite the most prominent example, had a different relationship to the secular state from that of the Protestants. This is clearly seen in the biases of the establishment of the secular education system, about which Gascoigne writes: 'there was a great deal of common ground between the state schools and churches, or at least the Protestant churches, as the Catholics constructed at great expense and with enormous travail their own school system without state aid.'[32]

Christian religious traditions were not alone in supporting the adoption of Enlightenment ideas in the colony. The rise of liberalism in Australia was not only driven by the theories of Locke and Adam Smith, but also by the British custom of free social and political institutions. The social and political tradition of England, with its emphasis on property rights, individualism and open public life, had a particular affinity with many Enlightenment ideas; so much so that de Tocqueville wrote that England did not need an Enlightenment because its public life was already open to intellectuals.[33] The tradition of a free England – an Anglo-Saxon freedom – fed into and was particular to the development of English liberalism.[34] This notion of being 'free-born' was used by early European colonists in Australia as a defence against aristocratically minded members of the colony and to agitate for rights.[35] Under the power of the early governors of the colony, no colonists had the rights of those living in Britain unless permitted by the governor. Even the locally born, nonconvict Australians did not enjoy all the civil and legal rights of a British subject.[36] The early struggle for rights in the colony was a struggle to continue the British tradition of rights – a demand that European colonists in Australia deserved to be included within the British political free-born tradition that came into existence before the Enlightenment. This struggle involved a commitment to British political tradition and, as Alistair Davidson points out, the notion that the colonists were more 'British than British' arose; an idea that came to manifest itself later in the nineteenth century as the assertion that Australia's identity was 'Anglo-Celtic.'[37]

While drawing on Enlightenment ideas and their power to challenge social custom, the political and legal structures of the colony were continuous with those of Britain. As Patrick Parkinson observes, the Australian legal tradition is a received English tradition and in fact had not developed into a distinct legal tradition even by the end of the nineteenth century.[38] The British Whig tradition carried over to the colony and at times worked well with elements of Enlightenment political thought such as progress, the rule of law, the division of powers and constitutional government. Wentworth's campaign for a free press, in the face of the view that the free circulation of ideas was perilous in a penal colony, derived from Whig political culture.[39] Richard Bourke, also a Whig, succeeded in gaining the increased freedom of the press, as well as the institution of a free jury system.

One of the British traditions that, at first glance, worked against Australia's consolidation as a modern nation state, unlike other nineteenth-century colonies, was the continuation of the tradition of the British monarchy. Governor Phillip, in particular, paid close attention to the rituals and formalities of this tradition.[40] But in turn, it was precisely the continuation of this tradition that served to facilitate the realisation in the Australian state of a particular kind of practical, Enlightenment vision. Gascoigne writes:

> There were the obvious obstacles of distance and colonial division, but in some senses Australia did not need the emotional apparatus of nationalism when that task was performed by the British monarchy. The result was that the various states, and even the federal government that emerged out of them in 1901, were regarded in much more pragmatic and instrumentalist terms. Government existed not so much to provide a sense of national sentiment and identity as to provide basic services.[41]

This state had a particularly utilitarian, service-providing role with a subdued nationalism, leaving plenty of room for Christian values to flourish. In this way, the continuation of the tradition of British monarchy meant that the late Enlightenment ideas of Bentham came close to being fully realised in the Australian state, which came to be viewed as 'a vast public utility.'[42]

Also heavily present in the British colonial settlement was the tradition of colonisation itself, bringing with it administrative practices and racial attitudes. Yarwood and Knowling observe that there was a similarity between the rationalisation and justification of the treatment of the Irish in the sixteenth century, well before the Enlightenments of the eighteenth century, and that surrounding the treatment of Indigenous people in the colonies. The English treatment of the Irish drew on the idea that one's racial origins could be overcome if English customs were adopted, a notion later applied to Indigenous Australians.[43] The accusations of barbarism and 'un-Christianness' made against the Irish were transposed centuries later on to Indigenous people (sometimes by the Irish themselves) to justify the dispossession and ill treatment of Aborigines in Australia, as well as of Native Americans on the Atlantic coast of North America. This view of non-Anglo races found support in the comments of leading Enlightenment thinkers, most notoriously Hume, Locke and Kant.[44] As far as colonisation formed sets of beliefs and customs in those who worked and moved through the British colonies, the traditions of colonisation itself had a strong presence in early Australian settlement. According to Yarwood and Knowling, more than a third of the military and naval officers, clergymen and missionaries, traders and merchants listed in the first two volumes of the *Australian Dictionary of Biography* had lived in non-European countries (apart from Australia) during their careers. The racial attitudes of people in the first and second ranks of colonial establishments were partly formed in India and other imperial frontiers.[45] This tradition of racial characterisation and treatment continued in Australia and served to bolster the dismissal of Indigenous tradition, lore and knowledge.

But not all traditions in the colony were supportive of Enlightenment ideas; many resisted, and at times prevented, the realisation of Enlightenment values. A number of varieties of Christian practice did not think that Christianity and reason were complimentary, and many, at the very least, thought that reason had to be bounded by religion. The idea that religion was necessary for social order and that reason alone was unable to ensure this was widely believed in the colony. The Evangelicals considered that discourse about the consonance of reason and Christianity was 'a possible distraction from Christianity', and Protestant Dissenters were wary of the antireligious overtones of Enlightenment ideology.[46] Many Catholics regarded Enlightenment thought as an infidelity. These concerns were often raised in debates regarding whether education should be built on religious belief. Some Anglicans as well as Catholics disagreed with the view that mental improvement would lead to moral improvement, and asserted the need for religious instruction to avoid the excesses of reason.[47] Catholic resistance to liberalism and secular education was especially persistent and, as noted earlier, with the establishment of a secular state education system, their insistence on church schools led to the development of their own education system.

Religious practices were not the only source of resistance to Enlightenment principles. At the same time as the unfamiliarity of the land drove a reliance on science to provide knowledge for agriculture, other characteristics of the continent and its inhabitants withstood easy incorporation into Enlightenment principles. Attempts to systematically rework the penitentiary institutions and introduce systems of classification and reward according to principles of human improvement were not sustained. In the case of prisoner reform, Gascoigne writes that 'the obstinate realities of human nature kept getting in the way'.[48] Any reform the prisoners experienced tended to be a result of the informality of the system rather than its formal practices.

Colonists and explorers were overwhelmed by the barrenness of the land, and the Australian continent was frequently regarded as the most extreme and strangest of all the colonies. The pursuit of progress through agricultural improvement was challenged by aridness and lack of technology in the colony.[49] Despite the faith in and effort towards improving the land, doubts remained about the capacity of the land to be improved, and concrete limits on agricultural improvement emerged. The foreignness of the Australian continent shook the Europeans' faith in the role of cultivation of the earth as a stage that all human beings were to acquire on the path to civilisation. As Kay Anderson comments, 'it was the outrageous oddity of a land where living things seemed to defy domestication or "improvement" – the practice that in classical humanist thought launched people out of nature – that fed colonial ideas about Australia's extremity.'[50] This 'extreme' landscape, however, was not always a matter of frustration. Alongside the predominantly instrumental attitude towards the land, a tradition of European admiration for the Australian landscape arose, accompanied by concern at its degradation and attempts at its preservation that went beyond the utilitarian.[51]

The early colonists' plans for 'improving' the Indigenous population struggled when Indigenous people resisted adopting European ways.[52] The early missions and experiments in education largely failed, and by 1850 most of the NSW missions had closed.[53] The ideas, values and beliefs surrounding notions of progress and civil society were seen by colonists to be held in little regard by Indigenous culture. The Reverend Samuel Marsden wrote: 'They have no wants, nor is it in our power to create any which will benefit them, […] they put no value upon the comforts of Civil Life, hence they cannot be induced to form any industrious habits to obtain them.'[54] Here we see the Enlightenment standard of a concern with material betterment intertwined with Christian tradition, as those 'who measured the capacity of the savage to receive the Gospel in terms of his response to material incentives' formed pessimistic views of the nature of Aborigines.[55] For example, it has been noted that ideas of property and linear, progressive temporality were not prevalent in Indigenous cultures, which were thus resistant to the British Enlightenment worldview.[56] For many Europeans in the colony, Indigenous Australians were an extreme case of humanity that refused to be easily incorporated into the European stadial view of social evolution.[57] Of course, the persistence of resistant Aboriginal tradition was not just passive, as Henry Reynolds has recounted. As they were increasingly attacked and dispossessed, the Aboriginal inhabitants of the continent mounted active, armed resistance.[58]

Not only did Indigenous peoples defy the Enlightenment view of their nature, but on occasion some of the colonists rejected it, too. There were some rare instances where missionaries and administrators did not hold a social-evolutionist view of Indigenous Australians. The Spanish Benedictine Mission at New Norcia, Western Australia did not demand that its Aboriginal residents abandon a nomadic way of life and adopt a European one. Gascoigne speculates that this might have been due to 'longer tradition of contact' with Indigenous people.[59] Governors such as Grey perceived 'that there was "some common flaw" in the whole project of improvement as understood by his contemporaries.'[60] Reynolds has recovered the various humanitarian traditions that argued for better treatment of the Indigenous population, observing that these were relegated to the periphery of decision making in the colony. The first criticisms of the behaviour of the colonists at the frontier of contact arose during the rapid expansion of the colony between 1824 and 1848, calling on ideas such as the common humanity of all men, Aborigines as the original proprietors of the land, and the need for compensation.[61] The same humanitarian tradition that had focused overseas on the abolition of slavery in 1833 became concerned with the treatment of Indigenous peoples. However, the colonists' crusade for development, with its emphasis on practical needs and colonial solidarity, drove a rhetoric that the only response to the recognition of guilt was to leave the country, which served to suppress the impact of such a humanitarian tradition. Humanitarian views were relegated to the sidelines of public decision making. By the mid-nineteenth century, as representative government and rights discourse in Australia increased, paradoxically there was a growing abandonment of the idea that humans were essentially the same and that human differences were the result of environment. Partly driven by the idea that Aborigines were 'unimprovable', there was a growing focus on a biological and polygenist paradigm for race with regards to the Indigenous population.[62]

The deployment of mostly British Enlightenment ideas served to bolster traditions or aspects of traditions congruent with it, while discouraging those traditions that were not supportive because of their incompatible and oppositional conceptual frameworks, beliefs and values. In doing so, those diverse traditions – both internal and external to Anglo-Celtic culture – were decentred and displaced. Enlightenment thought did not only brutally dismiss the worldview and ontology of Australia's Indigenous peoples, but it also existed in tension with many of the traditions of the colonisers. Not all traditions had a consistently supportive or resistant relationship with largely British Enlightenment ideas. Regardless of whether such traditions worked for or against Enlightenment values, or both, traditions nonetheless shaped the form it took.

Colonisation: Shaping an Enlightenment Tradition

The colonisation of the Australian continent, the particular configurations of tradition it engendered, and the continent itself accentuated certain aspects of Enlightenment thought – the instrumental and the pragmatic. The cautious Australian attitude towards rights and enthusiasm for utilitarianism partly reflects the specific tradition of the British Enlightenment. The Enlightenment in Britain took a more conservative form than the French Enlightenment, with the English lack of an absolute monarch to rebel against, the ability of intellectuals to speak freely, and a tradition of individual liberty.[63] Nevertheless, more radical, late-Enlightenment thinkers such as Bentham provided a distinctly English contribution.[64] But the more radical strands of the British Enlightenment were not centre stage in conservative British public life in the nineteenth century. They were more enthusiastically adopted and experimented with in the colony.

This resolution of Enlightenment tensions in early Australia in favour of a practical and utilitarian focus on progress is not surprising. Utilitarianism had a particularly close relationship to colonisation, not only conceptually but also in terms of James Mill and John Stuart Mill's roles as colonial administrators and Bentham's direct influence on settlers and administrators in the Australian colony. Conceptually, utilitarianism justified colonisation by arguing that the paternalistic colonial governance of Indigenous peoples was required until they matured and acceded to rational thought, civilisation and self-government. The pursuit of Indigenous people's own happiness, defined in utilitarian terms, then, was invoked to justify colonial dominance.[65] Furthermore, the Benthamite radicals such as Edward Gibbon Wakefield advocated positive programs of empire that were an essential part of industrial England.[66]

Strengthening particular strands of the Enlightenment tradition was one way in which tensions and contradictions across the breadth and variety of Enlightenment thought were reconciled. The direction Enlightenment ideas took in Australia not only assimilated or occluded some religious and other traditions, it also pragmatically resolved inconsistencies between conflicting Enlightenment discourses. While rights discourse played an important role in arguing against hierarchical tendencies in the colony and persisted as an influential discourse, its potential to disrupt the conflicting demand for social stability and progress meant that it was treated with some wariness, and sometimes sidelined as a form of radicalism. Rights arguments were tempered by an appeal to utilitarian principles. The demand to maximise production from the land through the establishment of large properties owned by few people clashed with calls for equality and the ideal of small farming settlements whereby the institutions of civilisation could be accessed by all.[67] Humanitarian positions towards Aborigines, supported by ideas about the equality of man and his rights, were limited by an emphasis on the (seemingly) incompatible obligation that the colony develop in accordance with Enlightenment ideas regarding progress and property. Like elsewhere on the globe, inequality was increased by a modern commercial society following principles of material betterment through improved political economy.[68]

Instrumental rationality took prominence in early European Australia. That aspect of modernity that helps keep the instrumentalism of modernity in check, critical rationality (among other things), had limited influence in the early years of European settlement. If modernity itself can be understood as a tradition, then Australia developed its own tradition of modernity with a distinctive structure of instrumental reasoning, which gave it a sense of continuity over time.

The Australian practice of Enlightenment principles highlighted some aspects of British cultural traditions and downplayed others. The cultural priorities of the colonisers were shifted by colonisation, and voices that might be sympathetic to Indigenous peoples were relegated to its margins. As Anderson has argued, the resistance of the Australian continent and its inhabitants to improvement according to Enlightenment principles came to have a deep impact on the European understanding of humanity.[69] The perceived extremity of the land and its inhabitants instigated a crisis concerning the idea that all humankind was of one kind and that there was an inevitable transition from the state of nature to civilisation. This crisis was resolved by the adoption of the view that races were biologically different. Ultimately, the Enlightenment principle that humankind was defined by its distance from nature and its capacity to be improved or civilised undermined the idea that all humankind were one. While, later in the nineteenth century, Darwinism theoretically led a return to a monogenist approach to race, the legacy of the turn to biological essentialism persisted, forever shifting understandings of race away from a paradigm based on ideas of civilisation. This loss of humanist strands of European culture not only impacted adversely on Aborigines, who in the twentieth century would face attempts to 'breed out' their race, it also meant the marginalisation of European traditions that understood humanity in ways incompatible with ideas of the material betterment of humanity through the application of reason and scientific method.

The Enlightenment tradition in Australia formed through establishing continuity and discontinuity with surrounding traditions. Nevertheless, this empirical entanglement of Enlightenment and tradition masks how, conceptually, the Enlightenment project of betterment struggled to acknowledge this relationship. The view that there is an acceptable place for tradition disputes the principles of modernity established by Enlightenment. Despite the interdependence between Enlightenment ideas and the configurations of traditions present in the colony, recognising that traditions were intrinsic to Enlightenment thinking in Australia calls into question its rationalist project and the modernity it initiated.

In the context of the Australian colony, we suggest that the inherent individualism and rationalism of modern government and public culture worked against the capacity to adequately address the roles of communal membership, the value of maintaining different traditions and, indeed, its own nature as a tradition. Customs could not be accepted on their own terms, but only in terms of a justification that cohered with Enlightenment thinking. For example, the Indigenous inhabitants could not be seen except in terms of a stage of development on the path to a European future. Muecke points out, 'as explorers and scientists, armed with this new theory [Enlightenment], arrived in Australia they discovered here a nature and a culture that they were constrained to see as ancient because of the conventions of their own emergent modernity.'[70] This limited capacity to openly engage with the role of tradition extended beyond Indigenous culture to the various other traditions present in the colony. Indeed, the colony itself was seen as a stage on the path from primitive to European commercial society.[71] Tradition, for Enlightenment thinking, can only be a way station on the path of progress towards modernity.

Conclusion

Valuing diverse communal traditions requires going beyond the terms and justifications of the Enlightenment framework and the modern social order it advocates. In John Gray's formulation, 'in the political theories of the Enlightenment, the universalist content of classical political rationalism reappears as a philosophy of history which has universal convergence on a rationalist civilisation as its *telos*.'[72] Through the application of reason, particular traditions are relegated to stages in the historical development of a universal political and social order. According to Dipesh Chakrabarty, it was this historicism that facilitated European domination of the world in the nineteenth century by positing 'historical time as a measure of the cultural distance (at least in institutional development) that was supposed to exist between the West and the non-West.'[73] By conceiving of human difference in terms of historical time, both the universalism of European modernity is achieved and the difference between the West and the non-West established. This understanding prevents the capacity to value traditions in their own right or, indeed, the concept of tradition in general. It defines tradition as 'outmoded', rather than as something that can trace 'its roots back to pre-colonial times' and that has a legitimate presence in the present and future.[74] To value a tradition in itself and to acknowledge that it might have a worthy future existence that does not lie in a rationalist civilisation is outside the scope of the project of betterment. To value multiple traditions is to accept multiple, alternative futures, undermining the understanding that humankind is heading towards a European modernity. Consequently, despite the influence of traditions on the forms of Enlightenment thinking adopted in Australia, their role could only be considered as fleeting and marginal – a passing phase.

The modern public culture established in settlement Australia, according to its own peculiar tradition, was a forum for deciding and debating decisions that saw only one possible future. In accordance with Enlightenment thought, the public culture established in Australia allowed for the challenge to and dismissal of tradition and authority through the application of reason.[75] By making debate on a topic public, the government and other authorities can be questioned and debated by anybody with critical ability. However, as we have discussed, the public sphere of modern Australia, by demanding that participants justify and measure themselves (epistemologically and ontologically) against the template of Enlightenment terms, or at least similar ones, delineated its limits in representing dissenting ideas and practices. Those whose traditions were radically dissimilar to and incommensurable with Enlightenment values could not be represented in public culture according to their own terms and values. The historical absence of a substantive recognition of Indigenous ontological belonging, for example, has been at the heart of Australia as an Enlightenment project. Moreover, its inherently antagonistic, modernist relationship towards traditions that were perceived as tradition meant that it could not openly recognise the role and significance of traditional communal groups in the colony, except as a stage on the path to civilisation. The future of the colony – to be decided in public debate – was a singular and rational one, only covertly shaped by the intricacies of tradition. This was the template of Australia's future.

Chapter Three

AUSTRALIAN VALUES AND THEIR PUBLIC CULTURE(S)

In Australia there is something of that past, you know, the fear that might have been justified at one time – 'this thing will fall apart' – it will fall apart unless you insist on a few concrete, easily innumerable values. And it becomes a part of your culture and mentality even though the situation has changed.

Interview with Ashis Nandy, 7 December 2007

In this chapter, we turn to survey the content of Australian civil society through a discussion of its public culture and sphere, identifying salient and predominant themes and issues. What we argue is that Australia is an unfinished project characterised by Enlightenment values that have become instrumental of pathologies of power. Contemporary Australian values have been and continue to be sustained through a matrix of power relations that were established through the installation of Enlightenment. Values that underpin national discourse have become pathologies in the way they have been invoked and applied through the dominant template: the rationalisation of tolerance, justice and equality for all, for example – as bedrock Australian values – has frequently produced its very antithesis.

The complexity of these power relations is expressed through a variety of social, political and cultural effects that are produced in the way Australian civil society organises, interprets and understands itself. This occurs in significant symmetrical and asymmetrical conversations located within narratives, both formal and informal, of Australian belonging. What characterises the substance of these conversations are contests and struggles about how Australia is defined, by and for whom. In the wake of colonisation's imperative – to alter and reject incommensurability (as we argued in the previous chapter) – the mechanisms, strategies and negotiations that form the basis of the Enlightenment society become crucial positions of national site hardening; that is, where structures and institutions are defined and codified. What informs and, importantly, acts as the decisive directive to the public sphere is a homogenous conglomerate of assumed (site-hardened) values that are at the core of contemporary Australia. These have been and continue to be resisted, however, through a plethora of responses created and circulated in the arena of public culture, now perhaps the most important place where pathologies of power are scrutinised and challenged, if not always understood.

In this chapter, we begin by providing an overview of the public sphere and its relationship to public culture. A crucial connection between the public sphere and public culture is examined through the notion of the Australian citizen and the sense of belonging or not belonging. Second, national site hardening is theorised as the means through which contemporary values become tools of hegemonic interests and continue an Enlightenment tradition that is pragmatic, utilitarian and instrumentalist. Third, an exposition on the 'other' Australia is presented. This is where counter-hegemonic values arise out of conversations in the public culture and where value-laden thinking is ethically questioned and understood. Finally, textual examples – published and filmic – are used to demonstrate the way(s) values in Australia are regulated, produced, represented and consumed against the dominant template of belonging.

The Public Sphere and Its Architecture

The public sphere is formed by and through the legitimated core institutions of a society. In Australia, given its status as an (unfinished)[1] colonial project of the British Empire, the basic institutions that were installed into its (assumed vacant) landscape derive from a value-laden framework borne out of industrialisation, colonialism, the consolidation of the national statist system and democracy – all imbued with British Enlightenment principles and thinking. Modernity in Australia has thus been constituted by the importation, assumption and triumph of the Western mind, both materially and cartographically. The subsequent spatial enculturation of and assimilation with this mind following European invasion and settlement of the landscape of Australia (so named through the colonial conquest), has inscribed architectures of public and civic consciousness that have marked or site hardened the public sphere in specific and contextualised ways. Traditions have been established over the past 220 years and more which support and perpetuate dominant ideas of national belonging, and of who is a legitimate Australian citizen. A dominant mythology has been installed which locates, through the logic of identity, essentialist notions of what constitutes Australianness. This is problematic for the way the national culture survives, as it is predicated on essentialist and psychological values and feelings that ultimately pathologise power through fixed notions of who should be granted legitimacy, or not. In Australia, the clearest evidence exists that demonstrates the effects of these power relations, particularly in relation to the Aboriginal population, their destruction through colonisation and their subsequent, systemic exclusion from the dominant narratives and institutions of belonging. As Danielle Wyatt argues, the building of the Australian nation historically has been intrinsically caught up in the powerful 'correspondence between the nation and the home.'[2]

Core institutions include education, medicine, religion (church), the media and the law. In Australia, these institutions have derived their legitimacy from the ongoing effects of Enlightenment thinking, particularly ideas formed around the individual in relation to equality, freedom and tolerance. One particular principle – justice – became entrenched as an Enlightenment orientation, derived from its inherent relationship to the powerful notion of civilisation, where the individual becomes the rational civic and civil subject. Overarching these ideas are instrumental national and state pathologies of power that have been evident in ideas and policies based, for example, on the supremacy of a white Australian space, realised through its culture and polity; a basic state heterosexist and heteropatriarchal duty and obligation; and the preservation of Judeo-Christian epistemologies – all for the purpose of a general assimilation of the other, and most frequently invoked in specific relation to, but by no means limited to, the Aborigine, the migrant and the refugee.

Twentieth-century Australia's public sphere was driven by two contradictory imperatives. First, following World War II, Australia modelled and benchmarked its core institutions consonant with the establishment of international human rights treaties, declaration, values and language. The entrenchment of a rights consciousness in Australia demonstrated the hallmarks of a rational, modern and civilised society. Through much of the latter part of the century, Australia prided itself as a beacon of human rights law and practice. The second contradictory imperative that emerged, and which complemented the human rights framework, was the entrenchment of the notion that Australia was a tolerant, fair and just society. Indeed, through political rhetoric, national celebrations and the creation of modern traditions such as Anzac, these notions became mythologised and rationalised as Australia formed and site hardened the content of its consciousness.

These imperatives have characterised Australia's development of its public sphere through the last hundred years and more. With the demise of the White Australia Policy in the 1970s, which was a direct response to the waves of migration from non-Anglo European nations and increasingly from Asia, Australia became a nation in which there existed two dominant forms of belonging. The first was based on the maintenance of the *monocultural* traditions of the core institutions. That is, it was acceptable and indeed celebrated to honour Anzacs with the phrase 'Lest We Forget.' This tradition had become a key site of

Australia's civilising *modus operandi*. Every statue and memorial across the nation dedicated to the Anzacs became a site of national self-definition, a cultural, political and social marker that mythologised a specific narrative of memory. This ritualised, cultural pedagogic and civic as well as civil act of belonging sits in stark contradistinction to the maintenance of other, institutionalised forms of forgetting. For example, and most significantly, the collective amnesia that existed regarding the effects of the colonial encounter upon Aborigines and Torres Strait Islanders is actively maintained through the polity's lack of will to come to terms with that encounter. This frames what could be described as a shared Indigenous and non-Indigenous trauma of belonging.

The second form of belonging that occurred cohered around the everyday experience of the *multicultural*, where the everyday exchange and interaction of cultural diversity was evident. Waves of migration, from the outset of the formation of the Australian state, have demonstrated this cultural diversity. Moreover, unacknowledged in the architecture of the public sphere is the fact that Aboriginal society itself was and is characterised by the experience of diverse peoples, communities and cultures. There was and is no monolithic Aboriginality. In relation to the remarkable demographic changes during the second half of the twentieth century, Australian society became explicitly a national home of substantive, lived and expressed cultural diversity. This form of belonging was recognised to some extent within the public sphere through the adoption of multiculturalism as a policy in the early 1970s. However, the dominance of monocultural ideology within the Australian political system prevented a substantial alteration of the epistemological basis of the core institutions, so that by the end of the century multiculturalism had become a suspect and diminished position. Although the national imagination had changed irrevocably, the project of modernity conspired with the establishment of monocultural borders, fixing the parameters of the public sphere. Traditions such as Anzac, nationalist jingoism such as 'We will decide who comes to this country', the government's rejection of the notion of the public sphere endorsing an apology to Indigenous Australians for the effects of colonialism, and the legislation to entrench heterosexual marriage in 2004 were all signs of a retreat from the reality of cultural diversity. Thus, at the 2005 launch of the book, *The Conservative*, the prime minister, John Howard, was able to rationalise that he was a 'profound opponent of changing the social context in which we live.'[3] For Howard, the viability of the conservative social context was through the maintenance of borders – physical, psychological, political, cultural – framed through specific (site-hardened) values based on a monocultural public sphere. Significantly, the rationalisation of these borders was legitimated simultaneously with the Enlightenment discourse on tolerance, a just society and 'a fair go for all'.

The Arena of Public Culture

If the public sphere contains the legitimised core institutions of a society, the arena of public culture forms the unfixed and uncalculated content of that society's consciousness. Following Donald Horne's[4] seminal work on examining Australian public culture, which highlighted the various cultural avenues of interpretation and self-definition that a society engages in – through its myths, rituals, festivals, legends and so on – here, the purpose of understanding the role of national public culture in relation to the Enlightenment project and the production of values in contemporary Australia comes into sharp relief. What characterises public culture at this time is that it provides the primary arena in civil society through which resistance and calls for reform can be expressed and where challenges to pathologies of power are possible.[5]

This arena includes the broadest ambit of communication and expression about who belongs and who does not. Public culture can be conceived of as the aggregate of mechanisms, contexts and spaces available to a society that provide the basis of communal self-understanding and self-definition. These mechanisms, for instance, can be found within the core institutions but are not limited to them; in this sense, any cultural form, artefact or practice can constitute an element of the public culture. From graffiti to the lyrics of a song; in marketing as well as through community organisations; through journalism and letters to the editor; in narrative product found in film, television, song, book, blog, YouTube or even government report; in everyday cultural sites such as cafes, sporting clubs, churches and mosques; with the ubiquitous mobile phone; on the beach – anywhere there is an expression and/or exchange of communication, it is evidence of the explicit and implicit consciousness of the public culture. Following the definition frequently provided about the role of the media – that it is society talking to itself – the public culture is constituted by a matrix of conversations of society: interpreting, producing, regulating, representing and consuming the context of that society. This forms the consciousness of a society.

Public Culture and Contemporary Australian Values

In contemporary Australia, the cultural arena is the civil space in which Enlightenment values are both embraced and contested. This is where the complexity of belonging becomes apparent, where we see Australia as an imbricated national culture: both a monocultural institutional society at the same time as being a multicultural reality. In this space, the dissonance of democracy can be heard and observed; it is also a space that nourishes cultural amnesia as well as ethical acts of resistance and reform. In Australian public culture, whiteness, heteropatriarchy and the monocultural are produced as well as resisted. But the true hallmark of public culture is that it is a space where the other can be represented and recognised. For example, while the public sphere may embed the instrumental nature of human rights through law and parliament, it is through public culture that human rights and their attached values and language about the vulnerability of being human are imagined, conceived and engaged with. Although the White Australia Policy has not been extant as a legal and political instrument of site hardening for over 40 years, its legacy continues through the culture of the core institutions and therefore in public conversations.

For example, Ien Ang has observed, in relation to the maintenance of what she describes as 'white fortress Australia' in both the public sphere and culture: 'what will undoubtedly heat up is the negotiation and contestation of the very meaning of the "Australian way of life", as its condition of existence become increasingly intertwined with the rest of the world.'[6] The debate over what constitutes Australian values has become a fault line in contemporary Australian culture and society. Events such as September 11, the Cronulla Riot in 2005 and the 'war on terror' have brought Australian values powerfully into the purview of politicians, political cartoonists and media commentators.

For the duration of the Howard government, a deliberate focus was placed on proscribing values that are related to a values sensibility for Australia. In 2006, this culminated in the release of a discussion paper, *Australian Citizenship: Much More than a Ceremony*, which outlined the basic tenets of what Australian values were and meant. At the heart of this paper, Andrew Robb suggested that these values included:

> [...] our respect for the freedom and dignity of the individual, support for democracy, our commitment to the rule of law, the equality of men and women, the spirit of the fair go, of mutual respect and compassion for those in need.

This typology of values is self-evident in a society that embraces cultural diversity and wishes to sustain and enhance its multicultural reality. They are the building blocks of a liberal democratic society. However, the Howard government, in contradistinction to these views, undermined their basis through support for a different set of values embedded within the Australian public sphere and circulating in its public culture. This bipolar approach to values continues to generate complex ramifications. On the one hand, Howard valued equality between men and women, yet discriminated against homosexuals. He valued mutual respect and compassion, but did not recognise Indigenous ontological belonging. This is where the Enlightenment project is fraught: in the absence of substantive support for the other.

To provide another example, the conservative journalist Janet Albrechtsen, who has waged an ongoing fight against a culture of diversity in Australia, maintained her 'fortress Australia' outlook during the Howard era at the cost of understanding complexity. Albrechtsen's anxieties are derived from a mindset that clearly creates borders between 'us' and 'them'; her views are rationalised again and again into the West and the rest. The intimate enemy for Albrechtsen is, in fact, the cultural diversity of Australian society, which disturbs and challenges her monocultural, monosexual and monochromatic worldview. In her world, there can be no borderland – undetermined and unfixed identity and allegiance, or in other words, ambivalence – but only borders and site hardening, 'set up to define the […] safe and unsafe, to distinguish us from them.'[7]

In a story on how to tackle Muslim extremists, she bemoaned the 'con job' of a national event in Canberra that brought together Muslim and non-Muslim Australians to deliberate on how to build bridges between cultures.[8] Albrechtsen lamented, 'We're fooling ourselves by imagining the problem will go away with a barbecue and a friendly chat over the fence.' For Albrechtsen, the values that need to be boldly stated and defended, dressed in the parlance of Western liberal democracy, are to be maintained through an attack on Muslim extremism. For her, there are no protocols of engagement required. Dialogue and notions of mutual dependence are redundant. In this sense, Albrechtsen makes a tyranny of Australian values. In her columns, the debate over Australian values is linked to the maintenance of a culture of whiteness, a culture of heterosexualism, and therefore a culture of exclusion. She wishes to 'civilise' Australia, to set forth a 'we' that shares certain beliefs, institutions and values. This resonates with John Howard reportedly saying, 'Australia's core set of values flowed from its Anglo-Saxon identity.'[9]

Albrechtsen has taken a strong position in defining Australian values. In her 'we', the core common values of Australia are conceptualised as heterosexual, and are rationalised in terms of family and marriage. There is no place for a sexuality (or identity) that is fluid or unfixed. She defends marriage as a heteropatriarchal institution which is crucial to civilisation. For her, gay marriage would be an idealistic experiment set to fail, just as – she argues – both multiculturalism and Aboriginal rights have also failed.[10]

These views provide an example of how Australian values have been essentialised and how the other has been brought into relief through their exclusion from the dominant narratives of belonging. Underpinning the basis of these narratives has been the principle of tolerance, one of the key discourses of civilisation. In its rationalised application, this principle has become a tool to manage and regulate aversion to the other. It both pathologises the other and normalises it at the same time. Tolerance, for example, has been invoked and institutionalised as a means of dealing with Aborigines and Torres Strait Islanders, as well as dealing with Asia. In Australia, tolerance is frequently articulated as one of its most characteristic values. For example, Prime Minister John Howard stated in 2006 that:

> In the twenty-first century, maintaining our social cohesion will remain the highest test of the Australian achievement. It demands the best Australian ideals of tolerance and decency, as well as the best Australian traditions of realism and of balance.[11]

The problem of tolerance as a value, however, is that – in regulating aversion – its realisation actually depoliticises those who are tolerated, and by its operation produces 'us' and 'them'. As Wendy Brown has convincingly argued:

> Despite its pacific demeanour, tolerance is an internally unharmonious term, blending together goodness, capaciousness, and conciliation with discomfort, judgment, and aversion.[12]

Australia's ideal of social cohesion, as it has been conceived and practised through most of the twentieth century and into the present century, is therefore inherently counterproductive. What is most striking is that the post-Howard era has proved little different in terms of how the nation is imagined, regulated and negotiated – all from the template of Enlightenment values and sensibilities, mapped on to an Anglo-Celtic social context. Despite a formal and historic apology to Indigenous Australians by Prime Minister Kevin Rudd at the beginning of his term, the modern fundamentalisms of Australian Enlightenment thinking remain entrenched – modified within a public culture that staunchly maintains borders based on racial and cultural difference.

Constructing or Negotiating Citizenship

The pivotal intersection between the public sphere and public culture in contemporary Australian society is the marker of citizenship. Following a broad theory of citizenship – that it is concerned with the relations between the state and the citizen, and between subjects and citizens themselves – the concept can be educed as both a formal and an informal process, which includes aspects of regulation, construction, negotiation and imagination. That is, in the public sphere citizenship is actively site hardened – constructed through nationalist and statist discourse. In the arena of public culture, citizenship expands to mean that it is negotiated through, for example, cultural, social, political, religious and sexual alliances and identification, which are both fixed and fluid, and thus context dependent. Thus, the notion of cultural citizenship refers to the *arena of culture* as a primary field of citizenship production. This brings into focus a tension between the subject as citizen of the state (with the requisite paperwork) and the subject as citizen of given cultural, global or social contexts.

The axis of the twin notions of subject and citizen(ship) is the person and where/how/why/when she or he is located in political, social and cultural contexts. Thus,

> [...] the subjective, interior life of individuals is subordinate to, and conditioned by, the public arena in which individuals relate to one another as community members. This subject-as-citizen approach puts a new complexion on the study of cultural practices, because it indicates that they are subject to change in the administrative policies of the state and its corporate institutions.[13]

Ruth Lister has further argued that citizenship is a contested concept involving 'a status to which rights attach or a practice involving civic virtue and participation in the polis.'[14] Implicit in these formulations are modernist notions of the individual and the play between rights and obligations.

As noted earlier, embedded assumptions in narratives of belonging lie in what is decided, legitimated, ruled and regulated by the dominant powers in society. Citizenships of belonging, both instrumentally and indirectly, are constituted through and against processes of hegemonic identity formation. For example, the essentialist ideas of who fulfilled the ideal of Australianness explicated in the Australian Citizenship Act of 1948 were based on patriarchal, heterosexist, Anglo-Saxon and racially embedded policies.

John Chesterman and Brian Galligan claim, 'Citizenship is at the heart of Australian politics.'[15] The history of citizenship in Australia has been one of exclusion(s). The primary conception of Australian citizenship has been derived from Anglo-Saxon Enlightenment models, which have resisted the changing nature of Australia from a monocultural society into a multicultural one.

Conversations in the Public Culture

Having considered the above background to Australia's public culture and identified key features in the construction of contemporary Australian values and citizenship, in this final section of the chapter we contextualise these concerns in relation to examples of narratives of belonging. First, a government text is presented that provides the institutionalised (public sphere) incorporation and dissemination of specific values to the Australian polity, which appear stabilised, fixed and monolithic. Second, three films are briefly referred to that demonstrate how the arena of public culture provides a crucial space in which communal conversations – collective, intercollective, subjective and intersubjective – can take place in relation to an ongoing negotiation of belonging.

What It Means to Be an Australian Citizen[16] was a formal document provided to new citizens between 1997 and 2006. Published by the Department of Immigration, Multicultural and Indigenous Affairs, the rubric of the booklet is 'Shared values for a shared future.' The main purpose of this booklet is to introduce an understanding of 'the meaning and value of Australian citizenship.' In it, the minister for citizenship and multicultural affairs at the time writes: 'Australian citizenship, like our Anzac tradition of mateship and commitment to a fair go, symbolises many of these values, including democracy, freedom and community harmony.' Throughout the booklet, the construction of Australian values is replete with images and symbols (both natural and human-made) that have become germane to the contemporary politics of belonging in Australia. The flag, the national anthem, the colours of the country, the Coat of Arms, Uluru, Aboriginal dot paintings, cricket, kangaroos and emus, the Queen – all these representations form a specific construct of Australian identity and the dominant narrative of belonging. Key values are underscored, such as human rights, fairness and equality before the law. All in all, the booklet is an example of the instrumental values that have been legitimated by hegemonic interests in the public sphere. What is of specific interest to the conversation it provides in terms of Australia's self-definition is that it cogently highlights internal contradictions within the polity.

The booklet actively supports the collective amnesia about colonisation and its effects. For example, the only representation of Indigenous Australians is in a traditional primitivist format, but more poignantly, on pages 16–17 – where 'the first Australians' are introduced – the depiction of Aboriginal society and culture is relegated to the past. Laid in bold print upon a sepia-tone photograph of Aboriginal men hunting, are words from the national anthem: 'In history's page, let every stage Advance Australia Fair'. This stark and anthropological representation of Indigenous Australian society completely undermines its value in the formation and present participation within the nation. The embedded hierarchical, Darwinist and racialised depiction of Indigenous Australians constructs a particular meaning of being Australian, which suggests that the nation is now post-Indigenous. This booklet thus frames Australian values through the pathologising of Aborigines as the past, as history. That is, the Aboriginal is *other* to the present. Nothing needs to be reconciled. This example demonstrates the construction of values through a core institution – government – where the very purpose of this document is to provide unambiguous, legitimised and stable content within Australian nationalist narratives of belonging.

In contrast, the films *Beneath Clouds* (Sen, 2001), *Floating Life* (Law, 1996) and *Head On* (Kokkinos, 1998) are all examples of how citizenship and values are negotiated, fluid and unfixed – that is, ever changing. The films each deal with specific contexts of identity and belonging. *Beneath Clouds* is a poignant story of two Indigenous teenagers, one visibly Aboriginal, one not. Using minimal dialogue, the film unpacks the presence of the colonial aftermath and its scars upon contemporary Australia, cogently saying to the audience that Australia is not a postcolonial nation, but one that is caught in systemic colonialism and attempts at decolonisation. *Floating Life* is about Asian migrants to Australia, encounters with a suburban landscape and the difficulties of cross-cultural and intercultural communication. Australia is imagined through a negative plate – as it were, an inverted representation of migrant settlement and negotiation of belonging in alien light and sound. The narrative unfolds from within the Chinese family; it is an encounter with an Australia that gradually comes into focus. *Head On*, the story of a second-generation, Greek-Australian family in Melbourne, focuses on the life of Ari, the gay son, whose sense of belonging and identity is played out amidst contests between normative and unruly behaviour and subjectivity. An acutely urban film, almost universal in its scope, *Head On* imagines an Australia that is distinctly unfinished, unknown, resilient and deeply vulnerable.

All three films demonstrate the ambiguity and ambivalence at the heart of Australian culture. The scars of racism, the attempts at connection and belonging, the pathos of inclusion and exclusion are all present through the narratives. These film texts are therefore contemporary representations of how the arena of public culture provides a critical, creative and crucial space for negotiating how to belong; this is where complexity is not denied, but actively engaged. The films show how Australian values are directly and indirectly formed, and show that there are possibilities to resist and challenge the dominant Anglo-Saxon, white, heterosexist and patriarchal legacies of Enlightenment Australia.

Finally, these films and the text examined above illustrate the challenges to belonging in contemporary Australia. Nationally imagined as a just, fair and tolerant society, one that has been built on a self-definition of specific events, myths, traditions and values, Australia reflects inherent contradictions within the Enlightenment project. Madan Sarup has argued that 'tradition is always being made and remade,' that – significantly – 'tradition is about change – change that is not being acknowledged.'[17] This is at the heart of Australia's ambivalence towards itself, evidence of which can be located in the interaction, expression and exchange between the public sphere and the arena of public culture where values are made – and remade.

Part Two

THREE MOMENTS OF THE ENLIGHTENMENT

Chapter Four

MOMENT ONE.
AN ACT TO REGULATE CHINESE
IMMIGRATION (1858): CELESTIAL
MIGRATIONS

Australia was not a voluntary kind of society to start with, a large part of it was enforced exile and that exile was justified in the name of criminality. There is always a kind of desire to abide and comply with – the tendency to identify with – the norms that have criminalised you and see another group as the ones who are really inferior and the really criminally indisposed. And it is almost as if you are turning against yourself and in being unable to bear the fact that you've turned on part of yourself, shifted part of the self-hatred onto others.

Interview with Ashis Nandy, 7 December 2009

This chapter presents the first of three case studies that illustrate the installation of Enlightenment values. In July 1858, the New South Wales Legislative Council appointed a committee to consider the provisions of a bill entitled An Act to Regulate Chinese Immigration. The bill had been the subject of intense debates that also coloured the broader maieutic horizons of the nascent Australian colonies and their later federation into the Commonwealth of Australia. In what has been referred to as 'the golden decade', 1850s Australia was a hotbed of factional interests through which the urgings of self-government percolated. Amidst the clamour for economic, social and political opportunity, there were both inclusive and exclusive attitudes towards Chinese immigrants. The responses towards the Chinese called on notions of British culture as well as Enlightenment ideas, deploying terms and structures for the public debate, which involved questions of racial and cultural difference in relationship to Australia's national identity. In the debate surrounding the Chinese Immigration Bill of 1858, we see characterisations of Asian arrivals as potentially detrimental to the colony despite evidence that they were model citizens – views that were later hardened into the White Australia Policy and that persisted in public discussion in the late twentieth and early twenty-first century on Asian asylum seekers and immigrants. Returning to the debate of the 1850s helps us see how our present responses in the public arena to racial and cultural difference are tied to ideas, terms and standards that were calculated and circulated, but not always settled, in the past.

Golden Hordes[1]

The first Chinese to come to Australia after the British government had claimed sovereignty, were indentured labourers, or coolies. Their recruitment was prompted by a labour shortage in the burgeoning new colony that was compounded by the dwindling supply of convict labour, the breaks in assisted emigration from Britain, and the failure of attempts to install Indian and Pacific Islander coolie systems. There were a number of factors working against the adoption of Indian and Pacific Islander coolie labour in the Australian colonies. The concept of indentured labour was problematic in a climate of antislavery, and cheap indentured labour also threatened to compete with a working class intent on preserving or advancing its rates of pay. In addition, the issue of race and the maintenance of a white population was of intense concern in a colony bent on maintaining British culture and traditions. Those who protested against the importation of Indian and Pacific Islander labour also railed against Chinese coolie immigration, circulating their views throughout the colony in colonial dispatches, newspapers, legislatures and special committees of inquiry. Chinese coolie immigration was brief and, with the discovery of gold in NSW and Victoria in 1851, the focus of concern about Chinese immigration shifted to new and turbulent frontiers.

Despite the misgivings of some, the allure of gold touched the imagination of many, and in the feverish rush to the Australian goldfields the population swelled with thousands of hopeful diggers. Friedrich Engels wrote to his friend, Karl Marx, that the Australian gold strikes had the potential to turn the world upside down.[2] Within Australia, too, there was a mass movement to the goldfields as hordes of people abandoned homes and jobs to seek their fortune. As the lieutenant governor of Victoria, La Trobe, observed, 'The whole structure of society and the whole machinery of government is dislocated.'[3]

The Victorian goldfields rapidly became the most popular, and in the first year alone of the rush, the number of ships sailing into Victoria more than trebled. Chinese diggers began to arrive in significant numbers in 1854, when the goldfields had lost some of their early shine. In that year, social turmoil erupted in a miners' rebellion, later known as the Eureka Stockade, with miners opposing the harsh taxation measures and collectively demanding democratic reform. Although this movement was not concerned with racial divisions, the Eureka flag subsequently made its way into the banner of the Anti-Chinese League, and was more recently unfurled by the Australian Youth League during the Cronulla Riot of 2005.

Antagonism towards the Chinese on the goldfields erupted, and in response to the Eureka rebellion, the Victorian government was quick to problematise the Chinese presence and legislate for their restriction.[4] In 1855, when An Act to Make Provision for Certain Immigrants was passed, the Chinese population of Victoria had increased from around 2,000 the year before to about 17,000, and was largely concentrated in the goldfields. The act was designed to restrict the number of Chinese passengers in any vessel, and imposed a tax of ten pounds for each Chinese passenger, to be used for 'the relief, support and maintenance of such immigrants.'[5] The hefty tax was used to control and harass the Chinese, who were organised into separate villages under the supervision of 'Protectors.'[6] The tax did not initially succeed in restricting the number of Chinese entering Victoria, who instead began to disembark in South Australia and New South Wales, from where they made the arduous cross-country journey over the border.

Violence continued to flare on the Victorian goldfields, with rioters assaulting and killing the Chinese in their attempts to drive them out. In their efforts to respond to the unrest, and to further regulate the Chinese, the Victorian government urged the South Australian and NSW governments to 'join in this same mode of exclusion' and pass similar acts restricting Chinese immigration.[7] By now, although the Chinese population in Victoria was approaching the 40,000 peak recorded in 1858, in NSW the numbers were much lower, slower to increase and not regarded as particularly problematic.[8] But this was not the only reason why the discussions and restrictive measures in the NSW legislature appeared less frantic and more calmly deliberated than in Victoria. As Charles Price comments in his book, *The Great White Walls Are Built*,

> The elder colony, founded nearly fifty years before Victoria or South Australia, had a longer established population, a more experienced body of administrators and councillors, and – forged in the furnace of campaigns against convicts and autocratic governments – a longer tradition of political manoeuvring and public debate [...] Moreover, some men [...] had been grappling with the problem of Asian immigration since the 1836 proposals to import Indian labourers, and could see matters in a longer, cooler perspective.[9]

Nevertheless, the NSW legislation to restrict Chinese immigration, finally passed in 1861, was the outcome of complex and often violent negotiations about the meanings of the Chinese presence in NSW and Australia.

New South Wales and the Bill

In 1858, when the bill to restrict Chinese immigration was introduced, the NSW bicameral legislature had been established for two years and was about to enact electoral reforms that would radicalise Australian democratic institutions well beyond the state of parliamentary democracy in the 'mother country' at the time. The NSW bicameral legislature consisted of a Legislative Council – whose members were nominated by the imperial governor of the colony – and a Legislative Assembly that was voted into office. The property qualifications necessary for British parliamentary office were no longer required for membership of the Legislative Council, and any voter was eligible for office in the Legislative Assembly. With the introduction of the secret ballot and the vote for all men over 21 either born in the colony or naturalised, an expanded sense of political power was emerging in NSW, causing new tensions to emerge between an emboldened, democratically elected Legislative Assembly and the older, appointed membership of the Legislative Council.

The Chinese immigration bill provided that no ship would be allowed more than one Chinese passenger per two tons, and imposed a tax of three pounds per Chinese passenger. Even before making its way to the Legislative Council, the bill was subject to lengthy debate, despite Charles Cowper (leader of the Liberal Coalition government) urging its immediate action. Cowper outlined two concerns the bill sought to address. The first was that, due to the port 'becoming crowded with Chinese, disease or other casualties might arise, which would require that some regulations should be made.'[10] He thought the colony should prevent the 'mode of introducing these people who were brought here much in the way of slaves.'[11] His second concern was that, because 'these people did not contribute to the revenue of this colony in the same proportion as the European population', they should be made to pay a tax to cover the expenses of interpreters and 'other exigencies that might arise' on their account.[12]

Other members of the assembly were quick to force the question of motive, or what Henry Parkes referred to as 'the principles' of the bill.[13] Parkes asked if it was a revenue measure or intended to prevent Chinese immigration, for he did not believe it could effectively be both. Each principle raised different issues for the various commentators, but every member was anxious about one point: either now or at some time in the future, there could be too many Chinese in the colony. Here, then, the complex strands of an invasion narrative, already deeply inscribed in the drivers of colonial Australia, twisted their way around the question of Chinese immigration – outlining, as David Walker puts it, 'the power and influence of [the] conspirators and […] weigh[ing] the forces of national resistance.'[14] As evidenced in these debates, neither the nature of the Chinese threat nor the nature of the resistance to it readily assumed the homogeneity through which the colonising project justified its exclusions. If the Chinese were not 'money calculating Pagans' purveying 'the evils of moral pestilence', then they were – if present as a minority – 'the most quiet decent and sober of men, whose camps afforded an agreeable contrast with the Europeans.'[15] Nevertheless, waiting on the distant shores of the 'flowery land' (i.e., China) was 'the swarming hive of the human race' and an alarming 'facility with which it could remove its population to this colony' and change its character forever.[16] And the colonisers thought that Australia's character should remain persistently British, regardless of all the migrations from around the world.

The British culture of the colony was interconnected with and mutually supported by the Enlightenment structures and principles driving the colony's public culture and its institutions. The installation of ideas such as progress, education, equality and freedom was accompanied by the calculations and analyses of civilisational hierarchy, agreeably establishing British culture at its peak. The British did not allow this order to be challenged by a people such as the Chinese because, if they were contemplated at all, they were already judged as inferior. If the idea of 'taxing human flesh' was 'un-English' and 'contrary to international law', it was only because the English had never before contended 'with masses of Chinese landing on their shores'. The poll tax should therefore be completely prohibitive in effect, rather than 'a paltry rate' at which to sell 'the morality of the country.'[17]

The idea of a culture so ancient and different from the British, so capable of maintaining those differences in the face of poverty, hardship and negotiations for the necessities of life, threatened the colonial cultural consensus at the heart of its civilisational mission. It raised the possibility that the Chinese, who came from their own 'celestial empire' and engaged in the same search for economic (entrepreneurial) advantage that characterised the British colonists, saw the latter as morally and culturally inferior. The fact that the Chinese arrived on the continent later, or would often return to their homeland and family, hardly provided the laurels on which the superiority of British colonialism could rest. For many, nothing short of total prohibition of the Chinese could assuage these most primal of colonial fears. There were objections that the bill did not go far enough.

A modified version of the bill, increasing the poll tax to ten pounds, was eventually presented to the Legislative Council, eliciting strong comment from several politicians and the *Sydney Morning Herald* (*SMH*), which at the time provided daily accounts of parliamentary activity. The *SMH* acknowledged the importance of the council's role in reviewing bills passed by the assembly, and saw it as clearly necessary in this case. For the paper's own part, they thought it was their business 'to prevent, if possible, the adoption of unrighteous laws', and they launched an impassioned plea for the Legislative Council to carefully consider the necessity for the legislation.[18] The paper stated,

> It is humiliating to find that our legislators, upon the very first appearance of a people whom it is possible to oppress, heap upon them the fiercest calumnies, arouse the passions of the worst of people against them, insult and assault them, and make it part of political capital to have been foremost in a crusade so disgraceful to our Christian civilisation.[19]

These sentiments were echoed in the Legislative Council by Robert Isaacs, who believed the Upper House should restrict itself to the rejection or acceptance of the bill, rather than appoint a Select Committee or review 'any measure which had been adopted after mature consideration by the other House.'[20] He emphatically concluded,

> No ministry would ever be permitted to pass into law a measure that would have the effect of excluding from our shores any class of immigrants who sought either a permanent residence or a temporary asylum.[21]

Isaacs's speech, one of the more eloquent opinions voiced against the bill, called on the wisdom of the ancients, the wellsprings of Christianity and the 'Know Nothings' of American slavery and foreign exclusions. The bill, he said, was nothing but a vicious attempt to prohibit the Chinese, who could never pose the threat that some believed they did. Isaacs's convictions were based on his 'confidence in the physique and morale of Britons', the 'vitality in the Anglo-Saxon institutions' and the 'mighty river of Christianity', which were strong enough to resist risks associated with the Chinese.[22] If a threat arose, and he did not believe it would, Isaacs asserted that the superior race would rise above the inferior, as they always had; Rome had only been conquered by the barbarians 'when she had sunk into effeminacy.'[23]

As Isaacs's talk of vigour versus effeminacy shows, British ideas of racial hierarchies were sexualised, and the idea of a dominant Western masculinity pervaded both the institutions and discourses of the British nation builders. Indeed, according to some accounts, in Australia such racial prowess would be revitalised and renewed, far from industrialised Europe, where 'the old race [had] grown cramped and weary.'[24] Ideas of both gender and race were thus hardened in the colonies through debates like those surrounding the bill. The character of British masculinity, etched deeply into the colonial project and its defenders, provided what Walker refers to as the 'hard unyielding surface of resistance to invading Asia.'[25] But while colonial British masculinity was presented as tough and indomitable, the colonisers nonetheless saw themselves threatened by the

Chinese precisely because the latter were weak, effete and inferior. As such, they presented the insidious threat of degradation through contamination, and the vulnerability of the colony lay in its feminine aspects. Walker refers to the problematic status of women in this regard, who were considered

> [...] slow to realise the danger that the Chinese presented. Upper class women were easily flattered by the suave manners and elaborate courtesies of the wealthy Chinese [...] The message was clear: Asia would make inroads into Australia through its gullible and politically naïve women.[26]

It was the feminine elements within British culture that would allow its contamination by the supposedly effete and weak Chinese, and their resulting ascendancy would break the correlation between masculinity and domination.

The anti-Chinese lobby was not primarily afraid of the onslaught of equals (although some thoughts drifted in that direction), but rather the modes and manifestations of everything they constituted as inferior. The report of the Inquiry of the Select Committee, set up after the bill faltered in the Legislative Council, testifies to, among other things, the fear of contamination haunting the British sense of superiority.

The Select Committee

If there was an expectation that the Select Committee would confirm the worst fears and suspicions of the Chinese detractors, the inquiry must have disappointed many. The minutes of evidence gathered over three weeks of committee deliberations painted an almost irrefutable picture of Chinese 'model citizenry.' There was evidence stating that the Chinese were nonaggressive, clean, healthy, sober, and rarely smoked opium or tobacco.[27] And yet the profile of Chinese virtuousness seemed to be painted only reluctantly, more as virtue *in spite of* its Chinese bearers than because of what Chinese culture or traditions might bring to the human condition.

Victorian and NSW goldfields officials indicated that the Chinese on the diggings were peaceable, industrious and law-abiding people, working together mainly over the grounds previously worked by Europeans. The fact that the Chinese were less involved in pioneering or prospecting – even if, as Walter Brackenbury pointed out, 'they only want an impetus given them to make them so,'[28] – was cause for concern for some interviewers. If the Chinese only found gold that the Europeans would or could return to find at some later stage, then they could be seen as unnecessary for the development of the goldfields. But without more evidence against the Chinese, this was clearly not a serious indicator of the need for radical new legislation.

The interviews established that the Chinese both lived and worked separately from the Europeans, partly through choice but also because they were often compelled to do so. Peter Cloete, who worked as an assistant gold commissioner in NSW, stated that under the regulations the goldfields officials had sufficient power to regulate the Chinese, and the taxes already imposed covered the necessary expenses to do so. After further questioning, Cloete conceded that the Chinese could afford a further ten shillings per month as a special tax, and if their numbers greatly increased, extra police assistance would be required but there would be no difficulty maintaining control. In regards to the conduct of the rest of the digging population towards the Chinese, Cloete thought 'the feeling against them is one which will wear away as they know these people better.'[29]

It was estimated that the Chinese diggers probably earned an average of one to two pounds per week and spent at least one pound per week, which was 'merely enough to live upon.'[30] Captain Wolstenholme, the Master of the Mint, reported that the Chinese exported approximately 2.5 per cent of the total gold produce of the colony to China, and estimated that amount to be around 10 per cent of the Chinese income. The rest of their earnings were spent in the colony. And despite the impression that the Chinese were not extravagant consumers, as Brackenbury noted, when they can, 'they live as luxuriantly as any class of men in the world.'[31] The evidence in the committee's proceedings corroborated neither the contention that the Chinese were 'stripping the Gold Fields of their wealth, to the injury of the Colonists' nor the view that they did not contribute to the wealth of the colony.[32] The earnest prayers of petitioners, such as the miners of Meroo goldfields, could therefore possibly be answered, albeit in a different sense of the removal of the Chinese threat than that envisaged by certain miners.

A few questions about marital status and the frequency of marriage between Chinese and non-Chinese Europeans were answered to the effect that at least a quarter of the Chinese had wives in China and, of the very small proportion of Chinese settled in the colony, some had married Europeans. A concerned 'gentleman resident in Hong Kong' wrote to the *SMH* in response to requests for information about the Chinese, saying he had 'read with regret accounts of marriage between English women and Chinese in Australia'. While keen to 'preserve the Chinese from the violence and oppressive policy of which they have been [...] the subjects', the gentleman did note that 'one of the most objectionable features of Chinese social life' was the absence of many Chinese husbands due to work demands. He stated that he did not need to point out 'how unfavourable the custom is to morality' but added, 'let English girls know that if they intermarry with a Chinese in Australia, it is at this risk – they are probably marrying one who is married already.'[33]

Bigamy was an offence against the laws and morality of marriage and the family, but the fact that many of the Chinese had wives in China lent more weight to the argument that they did not, and could not, contribute to the development of the colony. For protestors such as the miners, who complained, 'it is manifestly clear that [the] intention [of the Chinese] is not to colonise', the solution was to put a stop to all Chinese immigration rather than to find ways of encouraging the Chinese to settle.[34] The prospect of the population of Chinese colonists growing larger through reproduction as well as immigration was almost unthinkable for many, not least because of concerns about intermarriage. As George Ingelow reminded the Committee, from his observation of Chinese intermarriage with Malay women in Singapore, 'of course the result is a cross-breed.'[35] For colonists anxious to preserve their sense of racial purity, miscegenation was an even greater threat than the sheer weight of numbers of Chinese that might press on the colony's shores.

Despite the superiority in numbers of the British and European colonists, for some, nothing but the complete exclusion of the Chinese could erase or contain the threat they posed. Indeed, not progress or Christianity, equality or democracy or anything else in the armoury of the anti-Chinese lobby could withstand the evils they saw embodied in the Chinese presence in Australia. The inferiority ascribed to the Chinese, their femininity, poor health and slavery, was a mode of destruction that knew few boundaries, a particular modus operandi with which the forces of colonial domination had to contend. The economic threat that the Chinese posed to Australian workers, for instance, was an effect of weaknesses attributed to Chinese workers. The low wages they received as exploited labour created resentment and fear that they were competing unfairly and depressing wage levels. As a result, the organised labour movement, which pursued equality and fairness in the workplace, operated to exclude rather than include the Chinese. Indeed, as one miner exclaimed, the Chinese must be excluded in order to protect the principles of 'equality, fraternity and glorious liberty.'[36]

And, despite such passions for equality, contamination and degradation was thought to emanate from the bodies and morals of those branded as substandard. With the advent of the scientific discourses that emerged from Enlightenment thought, the deviant became the object of scrutiny and classification, fixed by the gaze of scientists and pseudoscientists and set apart as 'unnatural.' The devil was in the details of disease, diet, defecation, drugs, death and sex, and the Select Committee brought their power as 'authorised knowers' to bear on the bodies and morals of the Chinese. But question after question revealed far more about the desire, bias, assumptions and anxieties of the questioner than anything else. This desire was to reinforce a certain order of humanity, to establish British superiority by naming, compartmentalising and disowning a lesser race.

For example, the committee's repeated forays into what was described as 'unnatural practices' – or, in other words, homosexuality – yielded little but the 'private impression' of Captain Browne that they did occur. Captain Browne remarked that '[The Chinese] bring a large number of boys with them which is rather a bad feature', but said that he had not heard any complaints from the captain or officers of the ships, and doubted they would tell him anyway.[37] Nevertheless, he believed the Chinese to be 'a class of people who are addicted to [unnatural practices]', and when asked what reason he had to say so, he stated, 'Well, I have been in China; but it was a good many years ago.'[38] In contrast, apparently the machismo of the British meant they were not susceptible to homosexuality arising among the concentration of non-Chinese males in the goldfields.

That Chinese homosexuality was not verified through confession or any witness statement did not alter the fact that the question of their 'unnatural practices' was already part of what Michel Foucault refers to as 'the discursive explosion of the eighteenth and nineteenth century' and the type of power that society was bringing to bear on the body and sex.[39] This type of power proliferated sexualities and surveillance procedures. Elimination or control of vices may have been the intention of various agencies of power, but with the entry of scientific thought, 'indefinite *lines of penetration* were disposed' and unorthodox sexualities multiplied.[40] Sexuality was only one aspect of the living body at stake in the modern mechanisms and calculations of power and politics. The medicalisation of sexuality was paralleled by and entwined with a variety of other responses to concerns in the colony about behaviour and health. The government was anxious to contain diseases such as leprosy and smallpox, as evident in many questions put by the Select Committee. Like the management of 'peripheral sexualities', the systems for the control and regulation of disease were also instruments of power.

In 1858, the concept of disease had not yet been strongly influenced by 'germ theory', but an idea persisted from the ancients that particular states of mind – as well as 'non-naturals' such as poisonous air and water, strongly associated with dirt and decay – tended to produce sickness.[41] By the 1800s, a notion of hygiene had taken hold and, as John Waller describes, the new 'gospel of cleanliness' was particularly evident in the British navy, which 'enforced strict hygiene regulations throughout its expanding fleet. Associated with insubordination no less than illness, filth was kept at bay through regular scrubbing, whitewashing, fumigation and the use of antiseptics such as vinegar.'[42] Dr Haynes Alleyne, the health officer of the Port of Sydney, was brought before the committee, and he distinguished the English immigrant ships by their cleanliness, remarking on the abominable smell of other ships, which he thought was due to inadequate ventilation rather than 'the arrangement of privies' or the overcrowding of Chinese passengers.[43] He thought that the ships bringing Chinese were cleaner than those bringing German immigrants, believing that the cleanliness of 'our ships' was due to the surgeons armed with the authority to insist on it.[44] In regard to the cleanliness of the Chinese themselves, he reported,

> They are very clean. In fact, since the reports that have been in vogue here as to their coming leprosied, and otherwise diseased, I have been in the habit of having them all stripped and of examining them; and I do not think I ever saw any class of person so clean about their skin, or so free from any kind of skin disease or dirt.[45]

Captain Browne thought that the ships not regulated by the British Passengers Act were excessively overcrowded and dirty, and that their frightful smell was 'like that of a slave ship on the coast of Africa.'[46] In regards to the personal cleanliness of the Chinese, he thought 'there is a good deal of oil and grease about them', because they probably saw 'very little water from the time they left Hong Kong.'[47] But, like Dr. Alleyne, Captain Browne was impressed with the health of the Chinese.

   Isaac Aaron, the health officer of the City of Sydney, had more to say about the cleanliness of the Chinese. He acknowledged that the Chinese could hardly help 'falling into filthy and dirty habits' because of the way 'they are herded together', and that he had seen them 'washing in the drainage water of a cellar, which certainly showed a disposition to keep their persons clean.'[48] However, Aaron thought the cellar water was very dirty, and in the lodgings (which he visited between ten and eleven o'clock at night) where 'they were packed together more like Negroes in a slaver than anything else I can imagine […] the stench from perspiration, and their want of personal cleanliness, was unbearable.'[49] And then Aaron revealed something that was seized upon and circulated around the colony. 'Within the last fortnight a number of them were located in an untenanted house […] and they were making use of a hole in the floor as a privy, and the whole of their *excretia* went into the cellar.'[50] The idea that the Chinese were dirty and odorous stuck as markers of inferiority, while documented problems with sickness among German immigrants were overlooked (for example, in 1855 one-fifth of one boatload of German immigrants died from various sicknesses).[51] The fact that the inquiry's interviews did not find the diseases of concern, such as smallpox, present in the Chinese community did not remove the apprehension that, as the committee chairman believed, stench and filth 'must have been calculated to generate infectious disease.'[52]

Frontiers are vulnerable to contagious disease, and in accordance with the logic of medicine at the time, segregation and sanitary measures were the obvious preventative measures. The inquiry's consideration of the compulsory vaccination of Chinese immigrants for smallpox was thus a strange turn of thought and practice for the 1800s. As Alison Bashford writes in her illuminating analysis of medicine, colonialism and nationalism:

> Vaccination crossed and dissolved the boundary between the clean and the diseased in an altogether different logic to segregation and quarantine. Moreover, in the colonial context, the 'foreign-ness' of these foreign bodies was not only a biological reference but often a racial reference, as 'lymph' (as the vaccine matter was called) circulated through many populations of children, literally linking them across the globe.[53]

The Chinese had been using inoculation as a preventative for smallpox for over a thousand years, and the British had learnt in the early eighteenth century of Indian inoculation practices and those in the Ottoman Empire. Unlike inoculation, which introduced smallpox matter into a patient, vaccination – as developed by Edward Jenner in the late 1700s – introduced lymph from a cowpox vesicle to prevent smallpox. The most common method of vaccination was through arm-to-arm contact, mainly between children, but the use of stored lymph from calves became more common by the end of the nineteenth century.[54] Bashford explores the numerous and complex lines of controversy that attended the practice of vaccination. Advocates for and against vaccination talked about its contagious mechanism and contaminant properties, discussing vaccine genealogy in humans as well as animals. This debate gained in vociferousness after 1853, when the possibility of compulsory vaccination emerged in Britain.[55]

However, in the proceedings of the Select Committee, the practice of vaccination and the possibly compulsory treatment of the Chinese were uncontroversial, except for concerns about the cost and logistics of implementation. Detention up to ten days was envisaged as necessary to carry out the operation. When that was put to Aaron, he replied, 'I think we have no right to admit them without it.' And as for the expense, Aaron stated,

> If we admit them at all, they would have no reason to complain if we took the necessary steps to ensure our own safety, nor would the colony have reason to complain of the expense, because the evils that would result from the introduction of contagious disease would be so incalculable as to overbear all considerations of expense. Besides the existence of such regulations would be very beneficial in other respects, because it would have a tendency to put a stop to immigration of this kind.[56]

In targeting the Chinese as a health risk, the health officer of the City of Sydney revealed the alliance being forged between science and the state. In the interests of preserving the health of the colony, the government contemplated interventions not only specific to disease but also specific to a group of people. Importantly, these proposed interventions were also implicated in the regulation of the colony's borders, which would later encircle the young nation of Australia, producing what Bashford refers to as 'medico-legal border control.'[57] The status of the body and the population thus became a matter of national sovereignty: as Bashford writes, 'the health of the nation – national purity – was pursued by government as a racialised objective.'[58]

The Report of the Select Committee

The Report of the Select Committee, delivered three months after its proceedings were initiated, made several observations and suggested some amendments to the bill. The committee concluded that, while there had not yet been the need to quarantine vessels carrying Chinese passengers, overcrowding should and could be avoided by limiting passengers according to space instead of tonnage. However, they noted that there was no law to regulate the conditions upon landing, and that the 'herding together' of Chinese passengers in 'ill-ventilated and ill-appropriated buildings' was sure to cause disease. It concluded that 'the filthy and dirty habits of [the Chinese] temporary occupants are amply proved in the Evidence'. Vaccination was recommended, since 'there is a strong feeling in China against vaccination; and the appearance of some of the immigrants shews that they have suffered from the effect of smallpox.' The committee acknowledged that the Chinese on the goldfields were orderly, industrious, obedient and trustworthy, but it also approved of further regulations for their 'control management and protection.' In the committee's opinion, the phrase 'born of Chinese parents' was a sufficient description of the term 'Chinese' in the bill. And the committee recommended that the clause precluding the government from granting naturalisation to any Chinese subject be removed.[59]

The report met with mixed reactions. The latest news from England contributed to some of the prevaricating in the council's deliberations. Referring to the peace negotiated between China and England, the chairman of committees warned that this was not the time to keep the Chinese out of the country, for the 'English had long been contending for the right of going into China for the purposes of trade – after war this right had been conceded – and more than this the Chinese were to forbear calling us by the ugly name of "Barbarians" in the future.'[60] Joseph Docker concurred, and added,

'The British had just now, at the point of the bayonet as it were, compelled the Chinese to admit them into China for the purposes of trade – why then exclude Chinese here?' But neither political expediency nor evidence that the Chinese 'were not of the vicious, abandoned character that had been imputed to them' could displace a fundamental prejudice at the heart of the bill and the proceedings of the Select Committee.[61] As James Thompson concluded, there were many reasons why he could not agree with the report of the committee and why he opposed a second reading of the bill, including the demonstrable fact that the Chinese were undeserving of the opinions voiced against them. Nonetheless, he 'was not favourable on general grounds to the introduction of any class of people but of European descent.'[62]

In the short term, the bill was thrown out, and for a brief time different constellations of 'Celestial' and colonial bodies could perhaps have transformed the national landscape. By 1861, NSW had passed legislation to restrict Chinese immigration. Many of the negative characterisations of the Chinese that emerged during the committee's proceedings – the idea of hordes of Chinese invading the continent, and the transformation of their merits into vices – persisted in Australian public culture. However changing and changeable concepts such as 'race' or 'nation' may be, they both arm social subjects with a cohesive identity. As David Goldberg writes, this is 'an identity that proves capable of being stretched across time and space, that itself assumes transforming specificity and legitimacy by taking on as its own the connotations of the prevailing scientific and political agendas.'[63] In such leaps and bounds (but by no means seamless continuities) the 'yellow peril' found its way from Charles Pearson's influential *National Life and Character: A Forecast*, published in 1893, to the vernacular of Kaiser Wilhelm. According to Pearson's gloomy predictions, the world was on the brink of disaster: 'year by year the population of the Celestial Empire increases', and 'Nothing but the vigilant opposition of the Australian democracies has kept the Chinese from becoming a power on that more remote continent.'[64] Australia continued its vigilance and, as John Kane notes,

> In the first Commonwealth parliament, Senator Staniford-Smith (cited in Gibb 1973: 117) argued that the admitted virtues of thrift and industry of Asians, transplanted into Australia, became economic vices, which "would cause an enormous amount of wretchedness and misery amongst our labouring classes [...] For these and many other reasons the people are determined that Australia shall be kept for the white race."[65]

Thus, although the 1858 bill to restrict Chinese immigration to NSW was finally rejected, this was not before it had led to established categories, narratives, terms and hierarchical structures that persisted in debates about the legitimacy of non-Anglo Australian citizens. In this case study we can see in the inquiry the explicit use of discourses regarding medicine and population management to discredit a non-Anglo-Saxon cultural tradition and to exclude people of Chinese background from Australian citizenship.

Chapter Five

MOMENT TWO.
CUBILLO V. THE COMMONWEALTH (2000): THE 'HISTORY DEFENCE' – STANDARDS OF THE TIME

> At the least, one can say that human beings are capable of using any ideology, any faith, any idea system, in the long run, for the purposes of dominance – in the long run. So no religion, no ideology, no idea, no social theory can claim to be paramountly and irrevocably immune to human greed and violence – let me put it like that.
>
> Interview with Ashis Nandy, 6 December 2009

Our second case study turns to the effects of how law and ongoing colonialism in Australia have conspired to produce scientific, historical and political discourses where traditional cultural knowledges and values are dismissed in a colonial context. In April 1997, *Bringing Them Home*, the Report of the National Inquiry into the Separation of Aboriginal and Torres Strait Islander Children from the Families, was released. The inquiry uncovered widespread allegations of physical brutality and sexual abuse, and found that the forcible removal of Indigenous children breached Australian laws and international human rights obligations. The Human Rights and Equal Opportunity Commission (HREOC) recommended that the Australian government consider compensation for those forcibly removed from their families, and formally apologise. The recommendation was disregarded by the Australian government of the time, who asserted instead that there was no 'practical or appropriate way' to address the recommendation for monetary compensation.[1] This disregard motivated a number of cases of litigation against federal, state and territory governments to make reparation for the practice and effects of the removal of Aboriginal children.

Court cases for nearly 2,000 members of the Stolen Generations in the Northern Territory were commenced in the High Court in late 1996 against the Commonwealth government. In the first case against the Commonwealth,

Kruger v. the Commonwealth of Australia (1997), Alex Kruger, George Bray and seven other members of the Stolen Generations claimed that their removal from their families under the Aboriginals Ordinance of 1918 (Northern Territory) violated their constitutional rights to freedom of movement and association and guarantees for the due process of law. The High Court decided that the government had the power to enact the legislation, and in this ruling the focus of judicial claims shifted to arguments about the lawful exercise of that power. In his comments for the ruling, Justice Brennan recognised that although the 'revelation of the ways in which the powers conferred by the ordinance were exercised in many cases has profoundly distressed the nation,' the misuse of power was not an indication of its invalidity.[2]

It was in the context of the Kruger decision that Lorna Cubillo (née Nelson) and Peter Gunner each commenced separate proceedings against the Commonwealth government in 1996, claiming damages for wrongful imprisonment, breach of statutory duty, negligence and breach of fiduciary duty arising from their removal as children from their families, and their detention. As the Commonwealth was the respondent in both actions, and evidence in one case was applicable in the other, the parties consented to have them heard together. The case attracted considerable attention because of the enormous historical, political and moral significance of the hearing. The Commonwealth spent an estimated $12 million on its own defence.

The dismissal of the case provoked considerable debate about the ability of the judicial system to respond adequately to the moral and political issues resulting from the removal of Aboriginal children from their families.[3] There was apprehension among both politicians and judges about judicial activism as well as concern about judicial conservatism, because the resolution of disputes is limited to accordance with the law at the time, rather than seeking a social or political solution to problems. Justice Merkel, when discussing the claims pursued in Nulyarimma v. Thompson (1999), pointed out that:

> In each matter the applicants are seeking to remedy wrongs of the past committed against the Aboriginal people. In some instances litigants, even where assisted or represented by legal advisers, have unrealisable expectations of the capacity of the law to remedy past wrongs. However, the Court's role is to hear and determine, in accordance with law, controversies arising between parties. It is not within the Court's power, nor is it its function or role, to set right all of the wrongs of the past or to chart a just political and social course for the future […] The role of the Court is to adjudicate upon those claims in accordance with law. In doing so the Court is to determine, in accordance with its judicial function, what the law is rather than what the law should be.[4]

There can be unrealistic expectations of the capacity of the law to right past wrongs. In particular, there are questions surrounding whether the judiciary can effectively settle disputes arising from colonialism while being, at the same time, one of its instruments. The common law of England was brought to Australia as part of the colonial project, along with Enlightenment thinking that sanctified the inalienable individual rights of liberty and property. Among its tenets, John Locke's premise of equality before the law remains a strong expectation, against a disparity of access to economic and political resources.

With the dismissal of the *Cubillo* case, concerns were also raised about the practice of history. The case raised questions of the past and its standards, with the Commonwealth using the 'defence of history' to justify the removal of Cubillo and Gunner from their families and communities. This defence relied on a historical consciousness that supported European authority. Cubillo and Gunner had to challenge the official version of history *and* colonialist historiography, including the latter's distinction between the past and present, reliance on written evidence, and focus on individual rather than collective memory. The conduct and outcome of the case raised questions about the nature of history as an academic discipline, about whether a court can make judgements about the past or the quality and veracity of historiography, and about the level of understanding of the discourse of history in Australian public life.[5]

Public assumptions about the practice of history have stubbornly continued to draw on notions of objectivity and the irrevocable separateness of the past. The principal elements of the ideal of objectivity include a commitment to the judicial qualities of balance and disinterestedness, and to maintaining a sharp distinction between past and present, fact and value, and knower and known. This approach to history sees different historians attributing significance to different events in the past, while the value of their interpretation is judged by how well it accounts for the facts. Historians themselves may have less confidence than the public in their capacity to play the role of a neutral judge, or in the ideal of progress in whose service the past is often summoned, but the assumptions of objectivity have remained remarkably enduring. This view of history, as E. H. Carr tells us, aligned perfectly with the empiricist tradition dominant in British seventeenth- and eighteenth-century philosophy.[6] The impact of the British Enlightenment and its ideas about progress, science, reason and nature continue to shape Australian history, whether we consider that to be 'the past' or merely records of the past established by professional historians.

This Enlightenment moment examines the thinking that informed the court when it considered the judgements made about the standards of the time, rather than the legitimacy of the claimants' case. The values informing those standards, such as the belief in progress and the use of education to improve mankind, were a result of the influence of the British Enlightenment.[7] We are focussing on the ideas and beliefs that shaped the judgement because of what they suggest about the ways in which the attitudes and values of many Australians are still determined by the past and by history. The first part of this chapter focuses on the conduct of the case, while the second part focuses on the relationships between law, history and colonialism that emerge from the case. In its treatment of protection and welfare laws as benign in their intent and consistent with the standards, attitudes, opinions and beliefs that prevailed at the time, jurisprudence served to legitimate ideologically, and rationalise politically, racial hierarchies in the public culture in Australia. The case draws our attention to the state's participation in racist exclusions, and while the judgement attempts to relegate such practices to the past, it serves to highlight their persistence in present practice.

Cubillo v. the Commonwealth

Employees of the Commonwealth government removed Lorna Napanangka Nelson (Cubillo) and Gunner from their families. The children were placed in homes run by two religious organisations: the interdenominational Protestant Aborigines Inland Mission (AIM) and the Australian Board of Missions (ABM), run by the Church of England. The government was reliant on missionary organisations to administer and staff reserves and institutions throughout this period. Cubillo and Gunner claimed damages for loss of cultural, social and spiritual life and loss of entitlements under the Aboriginal Land Rights (Northern Territory) Act of 1976 (Cth), as well as exemplary and aggravated damages arising from the Commonwealth's 'conscious and contumelious disregard for' or 'wanton cruel and reckless indifference to' their welfare and rights 'under the dictate of' a general policy of removing 'half-caste' children without any regard for their individual circumstances.[8] The closing submissions of counsel for Cubillo and Gunner laid out the basis upon which their case was fought:

> These cases concern great injustice done by the Commonwealth of Australia to two of its citizens. By the actions of the Commonwealth, Lorna Cubillo and Peter Gunner were removed as young children from their families and communities. They were taken hundreds of kilometres from the countries of their birth. They were prevented from returning. They were made to live among strangers, in a strange place, in institutions which bore no resemblance to a home. They lost, by the actions of the Commonwealth, the chance to grow among the warmth

of their own people, speaking their people's languages and learning about their country. They suffered lasting psychiatric injury. They were treated as orphans when they were not orphans. They lost the culture and traditions of their families. Decades later, the Commonwealth of Australia says in this case that it did them no wrong at all.[9]

Cubillo and Gunner defined their removal and detention as exposing a conscious disregard for their welfare and rights, causing them substantial distress, humiliation and injury. Against this, the Commonwealth sought to establish that the prevailing thought at the time was that removal from their families was in the children's best interests, and that this action was carried out within the ambit of legislation that Parliament is entrusted to make. The language of the law was thus entirely at odds with the way the claimants described the wrongs committed against them and, as a consequence, the case exposed the law's lack of connection with the human experience, and was therefore a missed opportunity for reform.

Cubillo and Gunner were removed under the Northern Territory's Aboriginals Ordinance (1918). Section 6 of the ordinance permitted the director of native affairs, a Commonwealth public servant, to undertake the care, custody and control of an Aboriginal child of mixed descent if, in the director's opinion, it was considered necessary or desirable in the interests of the child to take the child into care. The law permitted the director to remove the child even when this went against the wishes of the child's family. The Aboriginals Ordinance was repealed by the Welfare Ordinance (1953), which came into effect in 1957. Aboriginal people of mixed descent who were formerly 'Aboriginals' because they were so-called 'half-castes' were now no longer necessarily within the amended definition of 'Aboriginal.' All reference to 'half-castes' was removed, and the meaning of 'Aboriginal' was limited to 'aboriginal natives of Australia', people with one Aboriginal parent who lived 'after the manner of' Aborigines, or who were under eighteen and placed in the care of the director of native affairs. The shift in the meaning of the term reflects changes in policies regulating people of Aboriginal descent. These changes were couched in terms of a move from protection to welfare, and the formal adoption of a policy of assimilation, declared by the minister of state for territories, Paul Hasluck, as policy in 1951. In the Northern Territory report, which discusses the changes to be brought about by the Welfare Ordinance, the director of welfare is defined as having a specific duty in relation to the Aboriginal population 'to promote their social, economic and political advancement for the purpose of assisting them and their descendants to take their place as members of the community of the Commonwealth.'[10] Under Section 14, Aborigines could be declared wards, and be taken into custody or detained in institutions because of their manner of living, inability to manage their affairs, social habits, behaviour or personal associations.

Lorna Cubillo, née Nelson

Lorna Napanangka Nelson was eight years old in 1947 when Amelia Shankelton, superintendent of the Retta Dixon Home, took her from the Phillip Creek Native Settlement to Darwin with fifteen other children. The Aborigines Inland Mission of Australia (AIM) ran both the Phillip Creek Settlement and the Retta Dixon Home. In his ruling on the case, Justice O'Loughlin found that the evidence was simply 'too lacking for concrete findings to be made with respect to the reasons behind the director's decision to participate in the removal.'[11] The 'void in the evidence' meant that no finding could be made as to why the director decided to place Lorna Nelson in the Retta Dixon Home.[12] There were no records indicating that the Native Affairs Branch was involved in the removal, although whether this is because they never existed or because they were lost or destroyed was not known. The judge remarked that, 'One would think that a government department that was involved specifically […] in the removal of sixteen part Aboriginal children from their families would have recorded such a decision.'[13]

The Retta Dixon Home was set up on an unoccupied section of the Bagot Aboriginal Reserve, so the powers available to the director under Section 5(1)(e) of the Aboriginals Ordinance to 'manage and regulate the use of all reserves for aboriginals' would have included a power to 'manage and regulate' the operations of the home.[14] From the outset, the Northern Territory administration provided an annual grant for the home, but the superintendent and staff were judged not to be servants and agents of the Commonwealth at the trial.[15] The superintendent had 'substantial independence' in exercising power over all children in the institution.[16] Officers of the Native Affairs Branch made periodic visits to the Retta Dixon Home, and did not regard it as satisfactory for its 'inmates.'[17] They recognised from the early 1950s that the Retta Dixon Home was an unsuitable location for children due to its proximity to the Bagot Reserve, where there was said to be a lot of drinking and gambling.[18] The older girls at the home slept in a dormitory acquired from the army, and were locked in at night for their own protection.[19] Although the conditions at the home were not good, and in 'need of substantial improvement,'[20] Justice O'Loughlin concluded that, given the shortage of funds and building materials at the time, the conditions did not amount to a breach of any duty the director might have owed to Mrs Cubillo.[21]

Lorna Nelson's time at Retta Dixon Home was very unhappy; Justice O'Loughlin acknowledged that she 'craved for, but did not receive, the love and affection that she needed.'[22] The staff administered corporal punishment, and on one occasion a missionary worker, Des Walter, a practising member of the Brethren Assembly, 'viciously assaulted' Lorna Nelson. Cubillo said that children were punished with the strap if they spoke their Aboriginal languages – 'Our language [was] flogged out of us.'[23] Other ex-wards confirmed this use of corporal punishment. Justice O'Loughlin accepted that corporal punishment was used, but not that it amounted to flogging. He speculated that this punishment was a practical measure because 'children had to learn English so that there could be communication, by means of a common language, between the children and between the children and the staff of the mission.'[24] Justice O'Loughlin thus concedes the use of physical punishment as a valid tool for teaching and learning.

The judge found that Mrs Cubillo's sense of loss for her Aboriginal community and family came from the 'severing of her ties with her family and the loss of her language, culture and her relationship with the land.'[25] Cubillo was 'taught nothing about her Aboriginal background and had no opportunity to keep in touch with it.'[26] Discussing both Cubillo's and Gunner's case, Justice O'Loughlin remarked that they 'suffered trauma and shock when they were removed from their families […] [which] continued throughout the periods of their institutionalisation',[27] and 'they suffered severely during the periods that they were institutionalised.'[28] But he stated it was 'the removal and detention, rather than the conditions of the detention that caused their sufferings.'[29] This suffering was seen to shape a negative view of detention, and was cited to undermine the reliability of the plaintiff's memory, rather than to support the harshness of the experiences recounted. However, the acts of removal and detention 'could not amount to breaches of those duties [of care] if they were lawful exercises of that power', which – due to the evidence or the lack thereof – he concluded they were. The destruction of family and cultural links was seen as a *consequence*, not the purpose, of the policy. The Commonwealth and the judge both expressed the view that when Cubillo was finally released from the home, aged eighteen, she could have made more of an effort to resume contact with the family they removed her from and to find out more about the Aboriginal culture that her removal was intended to undermine.

Peter Gunner

Peter Gunner was born in 1948 in a 'native camp' near the cattle station known as Utopia Station. A patrol officer, Harry Kitching, recommended that the boy be moved to an institution if his mother, Topsy Kundrilba, would consent. Gunner was seven when he was taken by Kitching to St Mary's Hostel in Alice Springs in May 1956. Justice O'Loughlin found that Gunner's mother had consented to his removal for the purpose of him receiving a 'European' education. Consent was indicated by a document with a thumbprint that apparently belonged to Topsy Kundrilba, who spoke no English.

The treatment of the document indicating consent demonstrates the uncertain relationship between proof and truth on which legal decision making rests. In the deductive logic of legal discourse, claims to truth are regarded as deriving from the facts provided as evidence, such as the document with Topsy's thumbprint on it. Yet, as the judge himself pointed out, whether Topsy understood the meaning and effect of the document, or even if it was her thumbprint, was not clear. The meaning of the thumbprint cannot be fixed or known.[30] With the onus being on the claimant to prove that it was not her thumbprint or that she was not fully informed when she gave her consent, the inadequacy of the court's acknowledgement of the ambiguity of the document is striking.

Sidelining the question of the context of the document effectively serves to suppress the importance of the colonial context in which Aboriginal people were subject. The Aboriginal Protection Acts and child removal and institutionalisation provisions were based on the idea that Aboriginal people were not competent to make decisions about their own lives. Not only were there provisions for child removal and institutionalisation without parental consent, but there were also provisions to control almost every aspect of their everyday life. For example, 'protection' and 'welfare' laws permitted unpaid or underpaid Aboriginal labour, and the official appropriation of any wages, restricted Aboriginal use of space, particularly towns, outlawed acts that might lead to miscegenation, controlled the involvement of officials in Aborigines' criminal defence, and restricted drinking and drug and alcohol supply.[31] As Chris Cuneen and Julia Grix write,

> The idea that Aborigines would exercise any kind of informed decision-making was fundamentally alien to the racial ideology that underpinned protection legislation. To the extent that protection legislation made Indigenous persons 'wards of the state' in a legal sense, it also treated them as *incompetent* to make decisions about matters affecting their daily lives.[32]

The general assumption that Aboriginal people were unable to make decisions about their own lives sits tensely alongside the attribution of importance to a thumbprint supposedly indicating consent.

The language of the document was formal, and requested consent from the mother to her son being an Aboriginal for the purposes of the Aboriginals Ordinance (1918) and placed within the 'care, custody and control of the director.' It stated that she desired her son to be 'educated and trained in accordance with accepted European standards, to which he is entitled by reason of his caste.'[33] The submission from the Welfare Branch to the administrator stated, 'Because of his caste efforts should be made to advance his present standard of living.'[34] Justice O'Loughlin did not accept this as evidence of the pursuit of a policy based on race without regard for the welfare of individual children. The High Court had already classified the legislation as beneficial and protectionist on the grounds that there was a need for 'special legislation and special consideration for Aboriginal people.' There was no causative link 'connecting "race" to a failure to have regard for the welfare of children.'[35]

The judge found much of Gunner's evidence regarding events surrounding his removal and stay at St. Mary's unsatisfactory. However, he concluded there was evidence to support the assertion that children there searched for food in rubbish dumps, were not returned to their families for holidays, had little contact with children outside the school and lived in 'shocking conditions.'[36] Welfare officers at the time were concerned about the conditions at St. Mary's, and these concerns were well documented in letters and reports. The judge wrote:

> What it provided may have been better than that available for the part Aboriginal children in native camps. But that was not the test. St. Mary's was offering those children the opportunity to enter European society and to learn European standards.[37]

The judge found that St. Mary's failed in its management and its care for the children by not providing proper and adequate facilities based on the 'standards of the day.' This failure of responsibility was attributed to the director of St Mary's, and the Commonwealth was found not to be liable for the breach.

In bringing their case against the Commonwealth, Cubillo and Gunner acknowledged that the director had the power to remove children, but contested the use of this power, contending that he did not act in their best interests. The Commonwealth denied that it had implemented a general policy of removal, but also added a plea in its defence, claiming

> [...] that whether any exercise of the power to remove and detain the applicant by the director of native affairs (which is not admitted) was reasonable, necessary or desirable or took into account irrelevant considerations or failed to take into account relevant considerations must be determined by reference to standards, attitudes, opinions and beliefs prevailing at the time of its exercise and not by reference to contemporary standards, attitudes, opinions and beliefs.[38]

The judge did not find that there was a general policy of removal of Aboriginal children of mixed descent in the 1940s and 1950s, a conclusion contested by historians both at the trial and in the debate which followed the dismissal of the claims. The court did not accept historian Ann McGrath's affidavit relating to racial-purity policies in the 1930s and 1940s, although her oral testimony about community standards in relation to the removal of part-Aboriginal children was given over five days in the witness box.[39] Another historian, Peter Read, provided the Northern Territory Aboriginal Legal Service with considerable evidence supporting a policy of removal. Lawyers were uneasy about his use of the word 'argument' throughout his affidavit, and told him, 'It is for us to argue and for you to provide the historical facts.'[40] In the end, after hearing McGrath present evidence to the court over five days, Read found that his affidavit was not accepted. He was told it was 'not considered good enough.'[41]

Consistent with earlier High Court decisions, *Cubillo* treats Aboriginal protection and welfare laws as benign in their intent, and European standards as the ideal to which they were directed. The judge found that the 'integration' of part-Aboriginal children was based not on race, but on a sense of responsibility,

> [...] perhaps misguided and paternalistic – for those children who had been deserted by their white fathers and who were living in tribal conditions with their Aboriginal mothers. Care for those children was perceived to be best offered by affording them the opportunity of acquiring a Western education so that they might then more easily be integrated into Western society.[42]

The judge took the view that the Aboriginals Ordinance and the Welfare Ordinance 'are not to be regarded as examples of punitive legislation. Rather, they were intended to be items of welfare or caring legislation.'[43] Citing the *Kruger* judgement, Justice O'Loughlin found that the power of the legislation was circumscribed, in his view, by a requirement that it was exercised for the 'welfare of Aboriginals or "half-castes", rather than being punitive.'[44] This view assumes that the power to 'undertake the care, custody, or control' of children was dependent on the opinion of the director that it was necessary or desirable – in the interest of the child – for him to do so. Such confidence in the unquestioned virtues of European society underlay the policies of successive governments, and the court's judgement of them.

The main reasons for the failure of the litigation reflect major limitations in a legal process that relies on rules, procedures and statutes, embedded within an ideology with a set of values and beliefs. These reasons can be summarised as: the view that legislation allowing the children to be removed was in their interests and consistent with the standards of the time; the emphasis on documentary evidence; and the challenge of time, which meant that many potential witnesses had died and that the reliability of memory and the liability of others were called into question. Justice O'Loughlin found that the Commonwealth was not responsible for what happened. As Jerold Auerbach argues, the judicial process reflects the culture and ideals of a group, and the quality of that group's relationships with others. The legal system rests on impersonal contractual relationships, an assumption of equality for legitimacy, the designation of a winner and loser, and the abrupt finality of a legal verdict.[45]

The Judgement on History

Explaining the removal of children in a letter responding to concerns about the policy at the time, Paul Hasluck said,

> For many years past, under successive governments, the policy has been that, where half-caste children are found living in the camps of full-blood natives, they should, if possible, be removed to better care so that they may have a better opportunity for education. The theory behind this policy is that, if the half-caste child remains with the bush tribe, he will grow up to have neither the full satisfaction in life which the tribal native has nor the opportunity to advance to any other status [...] The purpose [...] is to serve the interest of the children and to give them the chance of living at a better standard of life.[46]

As Justice O'Loughlin submitted, there was, in the letter, an 'unstated assumption that the standard of life that would await the child would always be better than life with his or her mother.'[47] The letter also confirms community concern and disquiet about the forced separation of Aboriginal children from their parents, and indicates that everyone didn't share this assumption. McGrath gave evidence to this effect on contemporary attitudes to the policy and practice of the removal of children, which was accepted by the judge.[48] Despite this, Justice O'Loughlin accepted that there was a school of thought prevailing at the time that felt it 'was in the best interest of part Aboriginal children to assimilate them into the European mainstream.'[49] The judge thus accepts as inviolable the authority of European structures of government to not only make laws but also to set the standards of the day, and to privilege one version of history over another. Only one set of common and shared values is acknowledged for the past, and it is expressed by the 'actions of many men and women who thought of themselves as well meaning and well intentioned but who today would be characterised by many as badly misguided politicians and bureaucrats.'[50]

The court emphasised documentary evidence, favouring the writing and record keeping that is an essential component of colonial culture and the management of Indigenous peoples. While more than a hundred witnesses were named whose testimony might have been significant, approximately ninety of these people were dead, and the others were frail – unable to provide evidence, or not called.[51] 'Over and above the absence of these crucial witnesses', O'Loughlin lamented, 'was the total absence of any documentary records that dealt with the subject of the children's removal.'[52] The primary evidence in Gunner's case was a thumbprint, accepted as signifying consent to his removal and detention, although this could not be challenged or examined in the absence of any other evidence. O'Loughlin's solution to the difficulty of challenging documents in court when the author was dead was to consider any contentions raised about the contents of the document with regard to other evidence that would lend it weight. 'The line of documents compiled in the Native Affairs Branch' supported a positive conclusion that his mother Topsy had given her consent.[53] Yet government records, as Cunneen and Grix have argued, are likely to record that the practices of removing children will comply with the children's 'best interests' and will meet the standards of the time.[54] The gap between the evidence presented in official historical records and the accounts provided by Cubillo and Gunner exposes the limitations of the court's interpretation whereby one version of events, based on particular types of evidence, is authorised, and other knowledge is excluded in order to form a single view of what happened in the past.[55]

Throughout the proceedings, the 'tyranny of time' was a problem, but while oral testimony was questioned in terms of its reliability, the same level of concern was not applied to other primary evidence. Oral testimony has become a central element in understanding Aboriginal history, but its use still causes concerns among some historians which parallel those expressed in the court, relating primarily to the separation of past and present.[56] Documentary records are interpreted in the present, but memory can be dismissed because it is shaped by the present and affected by hindsight, not the actualities of the past. Even eyewitness accounts, such as Cubillo's, were called into question in court because of the difficulty 'for anybody to recall events that occurred so long ago.'[57] More significantly, the judge expressed concern that Gunner and Cubillo 'unconsciously engaged in exercises of reconstruction, based, not on what they knew at the time, but on what they have convinced themselves must have happened or what others may have told them.'[58] The emphasis of the court on documentary evidence and the reservations held about oral history present a considerable challenge for members of the Stolen Generations.[59] Likewise, historians subscribe to distinctions between different types of evidence, based on their proximity – as a participant or in terms of time – to the events, issues or people in question.[60] Such practices reinforce an empiricist model of history, bringing history into line with the law and drawing on their shared traditions.

While adhering to strictly empirical models brings history into line with the law, the court's sole reliance on an overly empirical, documentary approach to history points towards a significant difference in how the past is treated: the legal desire for finality and certainty is at odds with the contextual and provisional nature of historical inquiry.[61] According to Justice O'Loughlin, the prime issue in the case centred on the individuals involved, limiting concern to finding the facts about the personal histories of Cubillo and Gunner. He conceded there was great public interest in the case as a result of the HREOC report and support for a public apology and compensation for members of the Stolen Generations, but he resolved to limit the trial to the

> [...] *personal histories* of Lorna Cubillo and Peter Gunner and the policies and the implementation of the policies of the Commonwealth to the extent to which they concerned part Aboriginal people in the Northern Territory of Australia between 1947 and 1963 or thereabouts and affected the applicants.[62]

Little attention was given to the possibility that consideration of the historical context would provide useful evidence, especially in such cases where the record may be incomplete. The refusal of the courts to give any weight to communal memory and shared experiences places a considerable burden on individuals whose only records accorded legal recognition in relation to their childhood are often the records maintained by government.[63]

History and Colonisation

The commitment in Australia to an ethos of improvement of peoples through upbringing, education and the application of science is largely a legacy of British Enlightenment thinkers. Bentham's utilitarianism justified colonisation by arguing that the paternalistic, colonial governance of Indigenous peoples was required until they matured and acceded to rational thought, civilisation and self-government. The pursuit of Indigenous people's own happiness, defined in utilitarian terms, was invoked to justify colonial dominance.[64] The stadial models of human development of Hume and Smith, in which modern European society was considered the most advanced, were expressed locally in the idea that Aborigines were the base line of human development, a relic of the childhood of the species. The gap between Europeans and Aborigines was perceived in terms of an historical trajectory, and there was an expectation that they could be raised to civilisation.

The social Darwinism embraced by colonists in the late nineteenth and twentieth century was part of a broader discourse of racial extinction decreeing 'the demise of all who failed to advance into civilization.'[65] Humanitarianism became increasingly marginalised as power in the colonies devolved from colonial officials to local settlers.[66] The colonists' conception of Aborigines as a dying race placed them outside history, in mythic time.[67] Aboriginal people and their culture were consigned to the past and to the margins. Extinction referred exclusively to a 'pure race'; 'half-castes' were not included in this notion. By the 1930s, Russell McGregor claims, it was recognised that the population of Aborigines of mixed descent was rising, and not necessarily being absorbed into the white community. Assumptions that the Aboriginal population would eventually die out were demonstrated to be false by this time, and increased concern stimulated a growing interest in the circumstances of children of mixed descent.[68] The pursuit of their assimilation was another route to racial and cultural extinction.

Colonial cultures are founded on deeply racist assumptions, and history is a powerful means of legitimation and explanation. The past cannot be easily compressed into a balance sheet of rights and wrongs, an appraisal of where we have come from and where we are going. But the way we comprehend it and its implications for the future may be shaped by such a paradigm. The history of the Stolen Generations throws up a particular challenge for non-Indigenous Australians, who have largely imbibed Australian history from a non-Indigenous perspective. Racism is central to colonial discourse as a justification for conquest and the establishment of systems of administration and instruction. Australian colonial history, like the histories of other settler colonies, has explained itself to itself in part through the deployment of simple mythical narratives of development and progress, which the testimonies of the Stolen Generations in part dispute, but which the judicial decisions reproduce by limiting their findings to the inherited colonial legislation.

The mythical narrative was teleological and nonsectarian; it made a virtue of improvement and pragmatism, of practical responses rather than 'symbolic gestures', and of equality based on the premise of treating everyone the same.[69] Hasluck pointed to 'two characteristic principles of Australian democracy' to support his case for assimilation: equality of opportunity and the ideal of a 'society in which there shall be no minorities or special classes'. Enshrining this in policy, the removal of Aboriginal children was one part of the implementation of assimilation. Race-specific laws and discriminatory practices *at any time* are seen to threaten the narrative upon which Australian colonialism is grounded, but are justified in terms of extending the fruits of progress, defined as equality and justice and civilisation to all.

The revision of Australian history is a challenge to the simple mythical narratives on which it has been based, and is often seen as undermining national pride when it is conflated with imperial loyalties. Nothing has propelled historical debate and public interest in the discipline further than the revision of Australian history in terms of considering the crimes committed as part of its colonisation. Colonial history was an important resource in Australia for generating nationalism, based on a reinforcement of its success, its peaceful conduct and the improvements it brought. Indigenous memory has provided a powerful challenge to colonial history and, in the process, has challenged the extent to which national histories can provide social cohesion and unity.

Historical understanding has been crucial to successive Australian governments' responses to the Stolen Generations. The Howard government favoured a 'practical approach' to reconciliation rather than a formal apology on behalf of the nation. Prime Minister John Howard insisted, at the Reconciliation Convention in 1997, that this is 'because we believe it will bring about true social justice for indigenous Australians'. But he attacked those who described 'Australia's history since 1788 as little more than a disgraceful record of imperialism, exploitation and racism' as wrong, saying:

> Such a portrayal is a gross distortion and deliberately neglects the overall story of great Australian achievement that is there in our history to be told. Australians of this generation should not be required to accept guilt and blame for past actions and policies over which they had no control.[70]

The minister for Aboriginal affairs, Senator Herron, said that he shared Howard's feelings of 'deep sorrow for those who suffered injustices', but that it was 'important to accept that we cannot live in the past and we cannot undo what has been done.'[71]

The subsequent Rudd government apologised to the Stolen Generation in 2008 but did not offer any compensation. There was, and remains, debate about the adequacy of the apology, in particular regarding the lack of practical measures accompanying it and its stipulation that the colonial violence of the past should be put behind all Australians and resolved once and for all.[72] As Robert Manne has pointed out, Prime Minister Rudd's discussion of the 'history wars' displayed a lack of familiarity with that debate as well as with the events and experience of Indigenous dispossession. Rudd twice argued that 'a nation's history could be interesting even if no blood had been shed on its soil', revealing a temporary amnesia about the Aboriginal and non-Aboriginal deaths during the frontier wars that could only indicate a failure to take the matter seriously.[73] The notion that the treatment of Indigenous Australians can be firmly put in the past so that the nation might progress is bound up with a nexus of ideas about history, improvement and civilisation justifying the mistreatment of Aboriginal people. These ideas continue to shape our judgements of the past and its relevance to contemporary Australian society and its future. Notions of improvement, sameness and social engineering persist. While the objectivity of history has been challenged, litigation has provided an alternative forum for privileging and legitimising a single colonial account of history.[74]

The claim that the 'standards of the time' justified Cubillo and Gunner's removal from their kin and community legitimates the exercise of imperial power and privileges a particular colonialist historical narrative, at the exclusion of other values existing at the same time. It consigns history to empathy with the rulers. The notion that the past is over serves to obscure the colonial project at the heart of nation building. The inability of successful governments to confront the violence undertaken as part of that colonial project only strengthens the claim that this history cannot be relegated to the past. In failing to find a means to provide reparation for the treatment of Indigenous peoples, we expose our own immersion in the colonial ideologies that elevate and privilege the legislature and judiciary to act on our behalf and arbitrate our moral and historical issues. The removal of Aboriginal and Torres Strait Islander children from their families and communities was not an unfortunate, aberrant event in the history of Australia. It continued the exercise of colonial power through institutions deeply steeped in colonial traditions. This case study underscores the powerful notion that Australia is a land in a 'permanent state of decolonisation', as Ghassan Hage has argued. In the next chapter we move to an event that took place in Sydney more recently, in 2005, to demonstrate other flagrant contradictions that exist within Australian culture and which test the limits of Enlightenment values.

Chapter Six

MOMENT THREE. AUSTRALIAN LOCALISM AND THE CRONULLA RIOT (2005): THE 'BARBARIC LAW' OF 'HE WHO WAS THERE FIRST'

What the Enlightenment vision prescribes is a kind of 'minimum norms of civility' with which you can live. For the immigrant cultures, the Enlightenment vision is less of a threat in the sense that it is what minimally you will expect if a group of strangers – not sharing common values of culture – confront each other. I don't think that this compatibility between immigrant cultures and Enlightenment values has been really taken care of.

Interview with Ashis Nandy, 6 December 2007

Introduction

On Sunday, 11 December 2005, Sydney's top-rating primetime news led its bulletin by reporting an event that has provoked reactions that continue to ripple through Australian public life. 'It started out as a show of numbers by locals wanting to protect Cronulla,' the report began, 'but by mid-afternoon it had turned into scenes not seen before in Sydney: angry mobs, fuelled by alcohol, turning on individuals because of their ethnic background.'[1] The Cronulla Riot, as it became known, was described by the *Sydney Morning Herald* as 'Our racist shame', a bold headline that summarised one response to Anglo-Celtic settler Australians' abuse and violence directed at Australians of Middle Eastern descent.[2] For others – most notably the prime minister at the time, John Howard – this was a local disturbance with no racial undertones.[3] Nevertheless, the policy response to the Cronulla Riot has been to stimulate national questioning of the efficacy of multiculturalism, especially in relation to the presence of Muslims and people of Middle Eastern appearance in Australian public life and public places.[4]

Our focus in this chapter is not an analysis of the 'riot' itself so much as using the riot to frame an analysis of settler localisation – that is, of how Anglo-Celtic settlers have installed themselves as Australian locals. In particular, we will consider how it is that Anglo-Celtic settler Australians have been so successful in installing themselves as 'the locals' to the exclusion of other ethnic groups – including, somewhat paradoxically, Aborigines. By what processes has this occurred? In our examination, we will demonstrate how Enlightenment ideas of property have played a significant part in this process of installation.

The story, however, is not a straightforward one. As we have discussed, group identification is at odds with the Enlightenment ideal that the state has an unmediated relationship with each individual citizen. By focusing on the installation of Anglo-Celtic settlers as the locals, it becomes apparent that this colonial process is made possible by Enlightenment rationality, particularly in relation to the idea of private property. Meanwhile, the breadth of Enlightenment thinking that would welcome all groups into the public fold is constrained by what might be termed Anglo-Celtic traditions of *localism*. These traditions are founded on a system of 'born-and-bred' kinship which is far from rational and makes place particularly significant to one's identity, while also articulating that identity with a double sense of belonging: of fitting in and of possession.[5] And as this double sense of belonging is based on a kinship system, Anglo-Celtic ethnicity is implicit throughout.

In order to ground this discussion of Australian settler localism, we will focus on local language in the public sphere, particularly by drawing on representations of the locals in television and newspaper reporting of the 2005 Cronulla Riot. This language study connects with recent scholarship of English and Australian localism. The cultural geography of scale is also ever-present. The installation of the locals and of the Enlightenment in Australia is an ongoing project that has, simultaneously, broad-scale and intricate effects on the lives of its citizens and inhabitants. This is not because the processes of installation filter down from a national level to the lives of individuals, but because the processes are themselves simultaneously small- and large-scale. Thus, while this chapter attempts to examine the processes of the installation of Enlightenment values in Australia at the local level, it is the nature of scale that separating out processes on one level from another is a fiction that is a product of analysis and point of view.[6] For this reason, the chapter also emphasises the relationship between processes of installation at the local and national levels. When speaking of 'place', then, we are often speaking in the double sense of place as simultaneously local *and* national.[7] There is, of course, a historical aspect to this relationship as well, for the installation of the Enlightenment in Australia preceded the concept of Australia as a nation.

It begins with an empire, a fragile British colony, and a frontier that transforms the cultural landscape through the most local of human processes as surely as one foot follows the other, step by step, together with an arsenal of conceptual and physical tools of possession and colonisation.

The Local Context: Cronulla Beach, Sunday, 11 December 2005

The event that has become known as the Cronulla Riot occurred on Sunday, 11 December 2005, in the Sydney beachside suburb of Cronulla. It was not spontaneous. There was a fight at the North Cronulla Surf Club the weekend before. Subsequent media comment on radio and in newspapers in the week following that fight was accompanied by a rapidly proliferating text message: 'This Sunday every Fucking Aussie in the [Sutherland] shire get down to north Cronulla to help support Leb and wog bashing day [...] bring your mates down and lets show them that this is our beach and they're never welcome back.'[8]

The day before the riot, the *Sydney Morning Herald* reported:

> For [Cronulla local] Shaun Donohoe it's war, pure and simple, and it has been a long time coming. 'It's been brewing for years.' For another local [...] it's time for a showdown – though it's not about race, he says, just manners. 'They have no respect for anyone.' Angered by what they see as an aggressive invasion by youths of Middle Eastern background, these men say they have had enough. [...] 'They look down on our women,' he says. 'They don't really assimilate to our way of life.'[9]

A crowd of 5,000 gathered at Cronulla Beach the next day.[10] The events began amidst a festive though fiercely nationalist atmosphere, 'sort of like Australia Day.'[11] The Australian Broadcasting Corporation's weeknight current affairs program, *The 7:30 Report*, similarly reported that 'Da Boys', the Cronulla locals, turned up early and by 10 a.m. a party atmosphere was already underway.'[12] This celebration of Anglo-Australian culture was accompanied by defiant statements of Anglo-Australian possession: that common outdoor spectacle of the 'sausage sizzle', or barbeque, was accompanied by a sign reading, 'Free snags. No Tabouli'; people held placards reading, 'No Lebs [Lebanese]'; a young man with an Australian flag as a cape had the words, 'We grew here! You flew here! 2230 [the Cronulla postcode]' written across his torso; '100% Aussie Pride' was inscribed on the beach itself; and a banner was held aloft demanding that unnamed others 'Respect locals or piss off!'[13] Despite the festive atmosphere, the invitation to party was clearly not extended to everyone.

Around midday, the 'party atmosphere' turned violent. The crowd began moving along the beach, seeking out and assaulting men and women of Middle Eastern appearance with 'fists, feet, flags and beer bottles'. The menace was amplified by chants of 'Fuck off Lebs!' and the Australian sporting chant, 'Aussie, Aussie, Aussie, Oi, Oi, Oi'. At times, cornered victims were subjected to a chorus of Waltzing Matilda – 'the first time the unofficial national anthem has been used as a weapon'. Police and ambulance officers coming to the aid of assault victims had beer bottles and other objects thrown at them. By the end of the day, 13 people had been assaulted by the crowd.[14]

Suvendrini Perera has written wide-ranging analyses of the Cronulla Riot, an event which she describes as 'a performance of native-ised territoriality' by Anglo-Celtic settler Australians.[15] This 'watershed event', she says, played 'a key role in enabling and legitimising a resurgent border policing of Australian citizenship.'[16] Perera emphasises the iconic nature of the place in which this Anglo-Australian protest against a Lebanese 'invasion' occurred. Firstly, Cronulla's beachside location situates it on the border of the nation. Further, and significantly, commencing at Cronulla beach's northern extremity is the 'birthplace of modern Australia' – the Kurnell Peninsula, where Lieutenant James Cook made the first Australian landfall by an Englishman on 28 April 1770.[17] For Aileen Moreton-Robinson and Fiona Nicholl, this connects Cronulla inextricably with white possession of Australia.[18] Cronulla is read as a place at once local and national, and ordered according to a possessive logic – a hierarchical order of belonging in which white Anglo-Celtic males take top position. In their reading, the Cronulla 'Riot' is more in the form of a protest than riot, and is 'underpinned by a rationality of possession' aimed at restricting the diversity of who is understood and represented as Australian.[19] Beyond representation, the riot and the language that accompanied it in the media marked out spaces of Australian belonging according to gender, ethnicity and everyday practices and habits, or 'manners'.

For our purposes, we might make additional connections. The site of the Cronulla Riot, connected as it is with the 'birthplace of modern Australia', situates the locals as subjects formed amidst the web of connections that constitute Australian modernity. This web of connections includes the many legacies resulting from the translation and transportation of the British Enlightenment and of Anglo-Saxon and Celtic cultures to antipodean shores.[20] In the following section of this chapter, we will begin to analyse the Cronulla Riot in these terms: in relation to Enlightenment principles and to whom those principles apply, and to a British and now Australian cultural practice of identifying as a 'local'.

A Description of the Cronulla Riot as an Eruption
of Localism in Sydney Print Media

In Australia, the idea of being a local, despite its abundance in popular discourse, has until recently received little sustained attention.[21] The word forms part of the quotidian 'white' noise that is the soundtrack of everyday life. In vernacular use, the Australian meaning of being a local has a strong resonance with that which has spread out via colonisation from the United Kingdom, particularly England: it speaks of how a place 'moulds a particular kind of character', or of how place defines one's identity.[22] A more contingent and historicised reading, however – and the position from which we start our analysis – considers how locals '*make* place relevant to their identities in situated interactions.'[23]

The 'situated interaction' in this analysis is the Cronulla Riot and its reporting; that is, the riot as a national media event. As we noted above, Perera describes the interaction as 'a performance of native-ised territoriality'. This is supported by media reports such as that of the Channel Nine News, which portrayed the intent of the crowd of 5,000 as 'a show of numbers by locals wanting to protect Cronulla' from 'an aggressive invasion by youths of Middle Eastern background.' At stake is the issue of (who decides) who belongs where – an issue debated using terms in which the dominant position of the white settler Australian is already embedded in the language of identity and place, including that place called the nation.

By treating the Cronulla Riot as a media event, and by focussing on the appearances of locals in that event, we are provided with a rich matrix for analysing the dominant language of belonging in the public sphere. To begin with, it allows us to focus attention on the language of local belonging as it is shared by mainstream media organisations and their audiences.[24] Print media is particularly suitable for such work, as searchable media databases allow easy, comprehensive access to a range of publications. In the description to follow, the two daily newspapers in Sydney, the *Daily Telegraph* and the *Sydney Morning Herald* (which we have used to a lesser extent), provide the bulk of the data, with supplementary material from television broadcasts. In the section following this description, an analysis of the data on being a local provides a means by which various aspects of a dominant discourse of belonging to place can be understood and explained in terms of their function in the Australian public sphere: who it includes and excludes, and how it achieves these effects.[25] The obverse of this analysis, how Middle Eastern men and women appear in the same discourse, is discussed by a number of authors, and while considered here, this is not our primary focus.[26]

***

Figure 6.1. Number of occurrences of the noun *locals* in two major Sydney daily newspapers in the three-month period centred on the Cronulla Riot of 11 December 2005.[27]

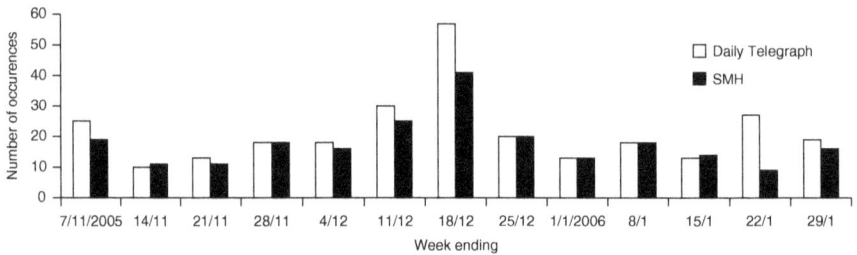

The link between the importance of being a local and the events at Cronulla in December 2005 can be most simply demonstrated with a histogram (Figure 6.1).

Figure 6.1 charts the number of occurrences of the plural noun or substantive form of 'local' in the two major Sydney daily newspapers, the tabloid the *Daily Telegraph* and the broadsheet the *Sydney Morning Herald* ('SMH' in the figure). Data was collected for the three-month period centred on the Cronulla Riot. In the year surrounding this date, the average occurrence of *locals* was 17 times per week in both papers. In this histogram, there are three main clusters where this number is exceeded. In the week ending 7 November 2005, locals of the popular beachside town of Byron Bay allegedly assaulted a major television identity, Rex Hunt. This brought 'locals' to prominence in the Australian media because, it seemed, the locals of Byron Bay were sick of tourists and outsiders taking over their town. As the *Herald* commented, 'the "Locals Only" sign etched with white paint on rocks at [a Byron Bay surf break known as] The Pass is a landmark. But the resentment is making its way from the waves to the land.'[28] A third spike in the use of 'locals' occurred late in January, when there was concern that there were no more locals – Australian players, in other words – left in the Australian Open tennis tournament.[29] These two examples indicate how the place of locals can be variably scaled. In one case, place is a coastal town (population 5,000, though hosting an estimated 1.7 million tourists each year), and in the other it is an entire nation. Both examples also indicate one type of situation in which place is made relevant to identity: being one of the locals is often invoked in instances where outsiders could be said to 'dispossess' locals of public property.

Of course, the most obvious spike in the use of the word 'locals' – of localism incarnate – was that which occurred in the three-week period centred on the Cronulla Riot. An analysis of data demonstrates a direct connection between Cronulla and use of the word. For example, in the *Daily Telegraph* there were no references to Cronulla locals during November 2005, whereas in December, Cronulla locals featured in 56 per cent of uses. By January 2006, Cronulla locals were again fading into the background, accounting for just 10 per cent of appearances. This outbreak of localism that started at Cronulla also spread to other locations, including the Sydney beachside suburbs of Maroubra, Bondi and Manly, and further north to Terrigal and Surfers Paradise. When this contagion is taken into account, uses of 'locals' connected to incidents at Cronulla accounted for 69 per cent of uses in the *Daily Telegraph* during December 2005.

In the week prior to the riot, 'the locals' was invoked as an expression of solidarity with the off-duty surf lifesavers from the North Cronulla Surf Club who were involved in the fight with young men of Middle Eastern appearance. In the days directly after this incident, the locals featured as being threatened by an increasing number of outsiders coming from the western suburbs of Sydney. The following two quotes provide contrasting attitudes to this history of social change:

> I have noticed a large increase in the number of Middle Eastern people coming there especially over the weekend. The majority of those people are really friendly and enjoy the area. There is a frightening trend, though, that younger males are becoming more aggressive towards the locals.[30]
>
> Sutherland Shire residents have tolerated antisocial and downright un-Australian behaviour from the influx of certain football-short wearing, gang-style riff-raff from the western suburbs for far too long. The suggestion now that Cronulla locals may need to travel to out-of-area beaches themselves, to avoid this ongoing harassment and violence from this group of uncouth bogans, is absolutely ludicrous.[31]

Already race is evident, with an opposition evoked between unmarked locals and 'Middle Eastern people': the locals are from Cronulla and the Sutherland Shire, while the non-locals are from the Middle East and the western suburbs. Similarly, this opposition is marked by a conflict over 'manners.' There is an unmarked rationality, which connects the locals to implied norms of sophisticated Australian behaviour. The non-locals, on the other hand, mark themselves out as unsophisticated 'bogans' (an Australian slang term for an unfashionable person from a deprived or lower-class suburb or area) whose aggressive behaviour is 'downright un-Australian'.

By mid-week, the historical sense of dispossession and loss locals were experiencing had transformed itself into action: a text message began proliferating between friends and acquaintances. This was the call to arms described earlier in this chapter. In the print media, the locals were no longer victims of an historic 'influx', and instead began mounting a retaliatory action to reclaim 'our beach' on 'Leb and wog bashing day'. As the text message circulated, a second fight at Cronulla Beach reinforced police and government fears that violence could occur on the following weekend. This threat of violence disturbed the connection between rational Australian behaviour and the locals: 'a beast surfaces' from the depths, as one headline put it. In the following examples from the *Daily Telegraph*, this disruption is rationalised via a range of discursive strategies: that the rule of law has broken down and that 'Middle Eastern gang' violence needs to be met with equivalent force; that individuals have the right to defend their common property; and, that all women deserve to be treated equally and respectfully. Overlaying these positions is the discourse of the state, which requires the maintenance of the rule of law and public order as 'the Australian way'.

> Racial violence exploded again at Cronulla beach yesterday [7 December] as a text message circulated urging locals to take revenge on Middle Eastern gangs. Police have [...] called for calm amid fears the text message's rallying call for locals to 'take back The [Sutherland] Shire' this weekend could become a flash point for violence.[32]
>
> [...] police yesterday [8 December] flooded Cronulla with dozens of officers patrolling on foot, motorbikes, horses, in cars and the PolAir helicopter, amid concerns a turf war could erupt between locals and gangs of youths of Middle Eastern background.[33]
>
> [...] only locals are capable of properly defending their beach.[34]
>
> Bashings by Middle Eastern gangs on Cronulla beach are not stopped by adequate police presence but when, understandably, locals try to do something about it, the gangs are quickly protected by police presence.[35]
>
> In the past, battles have been fought between locals and outsiders on city beaches, but this time it's clearly about race. Locals claim that Middle Eastern gangs overrun Cronulla every weekend, arriving by train and then gathering in groups to harass young girls. [...] The tribal surf culture in Sydney is all about paying respect to the locals. The beach is for everyone, but only if you play by their rules.[36]

In these excerpts, the locals' sense of ownership over public space confers certain moral rights. Such rights, as we will argue later, are rationalised via an Enlightenment understanding of property ownership, and primary amongst these is the right to peaceful and exclusive enjoyment. However, the tension at Cronulla arose when locals assumed a *private* right over the *public* space of the beach and its surrounds. The rules the locals played by, then, were not those of the state, though they intersected with those rules and were buttressed by them. Local rules are uncodified, so they are not subject to explicit definition, rational legislative scrutiny or judicial enforcement. Instead, they are inculcated through the processes and practices of cultural and social reproduction: something 'tribal' that is not solely the province of 'surf culture', but shared much more widely.[37]

Following the riot on Sunday, 11 December, the story being told was one overtly couched in terms of localism and locals. While the *Daily Telegraph* appeared to empathise with the locals in the week leading up to the riot by outlining the local point of view, after the riot a shift occurred. The empathy with the locals was maintained, but it was limited and localised in space and time. From within the local sphere, the riot was justified; from outside, the riot was viewed as an alcohol-fuelled aberration, an inversion of the rule of law with features of the carnivalesque.

The carnivalesque, according to Mikhail Bakhtin, may be understood as a 'temporary liberation from the prevailing truth and from the established order.'[38] Julia Kristeva notes that this liberation is also contingent on the acceptance of this temporary and alternative social code: the carnival only 'exists and succeeds […] because it accepts *another law*.'[39] At Cronulla, the official response to the riot was to maintain the established order by criminalising those who rioted and assaulted victims on the basis of race. This localised any racism to individuals, and enabled the denial of systemic or nationally pervasive racism. Meanwhile, the unofficial response to the riot in the media was to assert the primacy of order and the rule of law, yet also to accept the terms of the carnival, of the temporary but necessary overturning of state law in favour of the local rules. As Stuart Hall notes, the carnival always creates complex 'impure and hybrid forms.'[40] The equality of all citizens, regardless of ethnicity, is overturned by the carnival, yet Australian values of equality and access (to the beach) were emphasised. The use of the Australian flag (with the Union Jack in the top-left corner) becomes a banner ably representing this impurity: that is, of a diverse nation committed to the universal and rational ideals of the British Enlightenment under the southern sky, yet also proudly dominated by and rooted in Anglo-Celtic ethnicity and tradition.

As Rob Garbutt has argued, this carnival of the locals at Cronulla can also be read as the extension of an ongoing carnival, one that overturns the prior property rights of Aborigines and installs the locals as having moral priority as first possessors.[41] Again the overturning of the natural law of first possession is impure, though not disorderly. It operates around two axes: one overturns and one preserves. The first is a racialised axis that overturns the 'natural' order of Aborigine and settler, and installs the settler as native. The second axis preserves the order of indigeneity – of being authentically of a place because of being the first in that place. In *Hunters and Collectors*, for example, Tom Griffiths asserts that the 'white locals' are singing 'new songlines' with an 'historical consciousness that is Aboriginal in emphasis.'[42] This historical consciousness and these new songlines, Griffiths argues, are expressed in settlers' renewed interest in local and family history. And this expression is motivated firstly by 'the search for geographical identity – for "deep-rootedness"' that 'unravel[s] all the fine detail of their [Anglo-Celtic Australians'] attachment to the soil.'[43] Beneath this 'search for […] deep-rootedness', Griffiths contends, may be an Anglo-Celtic settler 'defence against modern inroads of multiculturalism and Aboriginal land rights.'[44]

Below are some excerpts from the *Daily Telegraph's* reporting of the locals' carnival, the Cronulla Riot:

> The day began as a show of solidarity with thousands of locals draping themselves in Australian flags and calling for peace in their beachside suburb.[45]
>
> 'I'm an Australian, I was born here,' a youth of Middle Eastern descent told locals who had taunted him with chants of 'Kill Lebs.'[46]
>
> 'This is what our grandfathers fought for […] we don't need Lebos to take it away from us.'[47]
>
> It was reported that a gang of Lebanese boys had forced locals away from the rock pool because 'Muslim women' were using it.[48]

As the days passed, public reflections on the riot began to reveal the complex and often contradictory logic needed to maintain the locals' rights to speak and act on behalf of the social space of Cronulla. There is a counterpoint between the rights of locals and the maintenance of the rule of law, and between a relatively homogenous community's attachment to a place through long-term coexistence and becoming a community open to being with others. In the process of public reflection, the theme that emerged was one of equality, though we sense that the appeal to equality *for all* and for the reasonable behaviour *of all* may actually be read as a case for reestablishing the status quo.

> Without further blame to those locals who did put on a very poor performance in the way they dealt with this issue, it should also be observed that blocking people using the local rock pools while ethnic women use them in religious attire is a very selfish snub.[49]
>
> But for all that, the response of Cronulla locals in the last few days to months – or years – of what they say has been a long campaign of provocation by gangs of 'Middle Eastern' invaders is dangerously misplaced.

They need to draw back, to take stock. […] It's time to allow the imposition of the law. Which brings us to the misplaced anger which has flared up in the Sutherland Shire. In this country, we have the rule of law and we all depend upon it. We expect the laws enacted by our elected representatives will be respected, that they will be upheld by the police and enforced by the judiciary.[50]

One of the many factors in the mix that has resulted in the Cronulla riots has been the misplaced and dangerous sense of 'ownership' that many locals seem to have of 'their' beach […] The problem is that this sense of ownership of what is public space is not all bad. It makes people feel they are grounded in a community and should take pride in where they live and look after it.[51]

It is not a racial problem, it is a behavioural problem, behaviour that is unacceptable no matter what your cultural background.[52]

Australian Localism and the Cronulla Riot

Press reportage of the locals at the Cronulla Riot expresses a number of aspects of Australian localism. Firstly, British cultural traditions infuse the idea of being a local, particularly the ideas associated with 'born-and-bred' kinship. Secondly, Australian localism articulates born-and-bred kinship with Lockean concepts of property rights. Finally, these aspects of what still could be characterised as British localism take on a particularly Australian character: namely, the locals' amnesia of their own history of migration, which in turn allows a process of settler indigenisation to unproblematically take root. This sense that the locals were 'always here' has a two-fold effect: in the first instance, it denies the public expression of Aboriginal dispossession in everyday language; and secondly, it justifies the defence of territory against newcomers – that 'barbaric law', as Adorno so forcefully puts it, 'whereby he who was there first has the greatest rights.'[53] As such, being one of the locals is part of what might be described as a 'language of Australian settlement'; a language that, despite the persistence of other, non-Anglo-Celtic Australias, is structured by a hierarchy of belonging to settled places.[54]

In this analysis, the ethos that is expressed through the Australian language of settlement is encapsulated in the idea of white 'autochthony', that sense in which settler Australians are able to speak of themselves unproblematically and assertively as the locals and as native Australians.[55] In saying this, we are not attempting to deny settler Australians a deep relationship with local places or the nation, but do want to emphasise the way these expressions normalise settlers within local places and the nation – the way, for example, the locals are always white, and Aborigines can never, with specific exceptions, be locals.[56]

The way, too, that – from the 1870s to the 1930s – 'Aboriginal native' was the term officially referring to Aborigines, whereas 'the word native [was] almost universally applied to white colonists born in Australia.'[57]

In his analysis of this latter language formation, Pal Ahluwalia notes that:

> The idea that white colonists born in Australia were natives whilst the indigenous population were not was an important one. It was an idea that went to the heart of the manner in which the continent was settled. The myth of *terra nullius* was dependent upon the non-recognition of the local population and the 'indigenisation' of their white conquerors.[58]

Proposing an Australian response to Mamdani's question for postcolonial Africa, 'When does a settler become a native?' Ahluwalia asserts that 'this occurred when white colonists were locally-born.'[59]

A key point in Ahluwalia's analysis is his assertion that being born in Australia was a precondition for the idea of *terra nullius* to take a place in the colonial language of settlement. In this understanding, the new land gives metaphorical birth to the 'white locals' whose roots are sunk deep into the soil, and this, it turns out, is a product of the settlers' transported British culture, specifically the born-and-bred system of kinship rearticulated with colonialism in a new land.[60]

This British system of kinship, which Jeanette Edwards argues might almost be thought of as a Western system of kinship, closely articulates being *born* – the 'immutable place of birth' – and *bred* – 'the effects of a variable upbringing.'[61] Thus, it is a kinship system that is both normative and symbolic: '[…] it is made up of a code of conduct (what people do and say they do) and ideas of shared substance (symbolised in idioms of blood and increasingly genes).'[62] Thus, in the site of Edwards's research, the town of Bacup, near Manchester,

> The statement 'Bacup born and bred' embraces two significant aspects of English kinship […] [I]t is not enough to be born in Bacup, one also needs to be reared in Bacup. The experience of being *brought up* in the town is said to be influential: it moulds a particular kind of character.[63]

Edwards's work clearly outlines the form that born-and-bred kinship takes, with implications for Australian identities. The place of being bred is thought to mould one's character (here the idea of the emergence of the 'Australian type' in the late 1800s is salient), and birth connects a person into a particular genetic and racialised lineage (an 'Australian type' born of British stock). At this point we might think of the man of Middle Eastern appearance who asserts to the locals, 'I'm an Australian, I was born here', before being assaulted for 'smartarse' behaviour.[64] For the Anglo-Celtic crowd of locals, this claim of being born here cannot be reconciled with being 'born and bred' under the Australian flag. A line in the sand has been crossed, a line of demarcation around being born and bred of the nation, and around being a Cronulla local that may well be to do with custom and religion, but undeniably has racial links too. The line that is crossed, however, is not expressed publicly in these terms. Rather, as born-and-bred kinship allows, the transgression which cuts a man and 'his kind' from the network of local and national kinship is expressed in the more acceptable terms of breeding, of 'manners'. The continual references to behaviour in the media indiscriminately set people of Middle Eastern appearance apart because they do not 'fit in' to acceptable norms of Australian behaviour. These norms are assumed to be universal, but are a predominantly Anglo-Saxon cultural construct.

Born-and-bred kinship's emphasis on 'fitting in' has additional consequences for the Australian settler ethos: a proprietorial aspect to identity and belonging. We see it at work in what 'started out as a show of numbers by locals wanting to *protect* Cronulla', and we read it in the assumption of a moral right to public space in the command to outsiders that they 'Respect locals or piss off!'[65] Nigel Rapport writes that, in the site of his fieldwork – the English village of Wanet – the locals have a sense of moral priority with respect to locality. 'Indeed,' Rapport says,

> [...] morality might be glossed as the rights conferred upon people by their local belonging, in particular their ownership of local land – their priority over land. What is moral in Wanet is [...] an absolute right to defend 'local' borders against 'outsider' trespass.[66]

For Jeanette Edwards and Marilyn Strathern, this articulation of ownership and morality is a product of a kinship system in which there is a strong normative element; that is, in which exclusion can result from not fitting in, even if there are blood ties. It is for this reason that they believe the idea of belonging is not a neutral term but, within born-and-bred kinship cultures, is a word with positive overtones or affect. That is:

> There is a moral propriety to the indigenous English concept of 'ownership' which suggests that it is as natural to (want to) possess things, as part of one's own self-definition, as it is to be part of a community or belong to a family. This gives rise to a proprietorial identity being claimed over a large range of animate, inanimate, and quasi-animate entities, such as one's own past, the place where one lives, inheritance, family

names, and so forth. […] Narrating such associations makes chains out
of them, and claims can travel along chains.[67]

The born-and-bred mode of ownership, then, has 'connotations of alienable
possessions and inalienable possessiveness.'[68] It is in this sense that locals can
make possessive claims that are based on social 'ownership' of a range of
items of significance, including a form of ownership of public land that is
outside property law. Furthermore, we could also propose that the locals'
claim over a locality is accompanied by a connected claim of ownership over
Australian identity. Ownership of Australian identity by the 'locals' of the
nation encloses identity for their exclusive enjoyment and allows them to act
as proprietorial gatekeepers. The Enlightenment idea of the equality of all
citizens within the nation is therefore loaded with a range of exclusions of the
locals' choosing. The normalised convergence between the universalism of
the Enlightenment and the parochialism of tradition diverges in this instance
to reveal the Christian tradition as the basis of full cultural citizenship in
Australia, together with Anglo-Celtic heritage – as opposed to Lebanese and
Islamic traditions, for example.

Meanwhile, although the locals' possessive claims to public space are
outside property law, they reside alongside and are reinforced by John Locke's
Enlightenment idea of property. If born-and-bred kinship provides deep
cultural and emotional soil in which settlers' claims of *terra nullius* take root,
Locke's concept of property provides the framework of support by way of a
legal and emotion-free rationale.

Kay Anderson provides a careful examination of the function of Lockean
property rights in the Australian context, particularly as they pertain to *terra
nullius*.[69] She notes four interconnecting assumptions underpinning Locke's
theory of land as property, of which three concern us here. The first was that
property and government were inconsistent with hunting and gathering. This
assumption was closely connected with the second, that 'property rights lay in
the products of human labour.'[70] For land to be property, labour needed to be
added to it, which – for Locke – meant clearing, tilling, planting and animal
rearing; hunting and gathering gave 'property' rights to game, tubers, fruits
and seeds, but not to the land itself. Locke expresses it as follows: '[…] Labour,
in the Beginning, *gave a Right of Property* where-ever any one was pleased to
imploy it, upon what was common'. Thus, '*as much Land* as a Man Tills, Plants,
Improves, Cultivates, and can use the Product of, so much is his *Property*. He by
his labour does, as it were, inclose it from the Common.'[71]

Locke's third assumption was that it was not necessary for consent to be
given by indigenous hunters and gatherers to colonists in order to appropriate
lands because indigenous peoples would benefit from the surplus produced

by colonial agriculture. A basic principle of Western law, the right of first possession, is overturned by arguing that hunters and gatherers do not possess the land, and that if any moral doubt remains regarding the colonial act of displacement, they will be better off when the land is cultivated by others.[72] Indeed, the idea of 'betterment' – whether of the lot of individuals or of the land – underlies Locke's reasoning. When Peter Read examines rural Australians' connections to the land in his book, *Belonging*, he neatly and perhaps unconsciously sums up Locke's idea of land and property:

> My feeling is growing that the once implied and now explicit Aboriginal moral claim to the land perhaps is answered, not by contentious or aggressive assertion, but by a statement of countering values. [...] The moral justification is evolving through a three-way relationship between a man, his work and the land.[73]

There are, then, complex cultural and legal–rational buttresses that, together, support Anglo-Celtic settlers' localisation on the Australian land mass. The result is the locals' sense of possession of the settled spaces of Australia, which justifies the morality of speaking and acting for places, whether at the national or the local level. Specifically, we have described three key elements. The establishment of Australia as a British colony installed a Lockean regime of property rights that was protected and enforced by colonial and, later, by postcolonial governments. Alongside this, British settlers brought with them a transplanted system of born-and-bred kinship that intimately connects people and identity to local and national places of their birth. This enabled the children of colonists to forget their history of migration, dislocation and colonial dispossession, and – as *settlers* – to install themselves as the locals, who have always been here. Between a legal–rational framework of property rights and cultural practices connecting people and places, the locals undergo a process of 'indigenisation' which enables them to claim the rights as first possessors of the land over the rights of migrants who come later and are of different blood and breeding.

Concomitantly, if they hadn't felt it before, those people of Middle Eastern appearance who were involved in the Cronulla Riot experienced a different trauma of dispossession. The statement, 'I'm an Australian, I was born here', are the words of a person who finds himself an unrecognisable Australian in the eyes of the locals: he is simultaneously in the land of his birth and in a foreign country. Equality, in its informal sense, is no longer guaranteed in public spaces when the 'locals' enforce their local rules and traditions. The individual who is no longer deemed to fit in is laid bare before the crowd, marked by his difference.

Conclusion

The contradictory logic by which born-and-bred Anglo-Celtic Australians claim to have always come from here, and not to be products of migration, is beginning to unravel. The children of non-Anglo-Celtic migrants unsettle the idea of the born-and-bred Australian having British heritage and observing the Christian tradition. When a young person of 'Middle Eastern appearance' confronts his peers with, 'I'm an Australian, I was born here', the born-and-bred logic of who is a local and who is not is no longer a homogenising force, but a fragmenting one. When Aborigines and Torres Strait Islanders demonstrate in law their claims of land as property, and therefore reestablish the rights of first possession, the ground on which the carnival of the locals is erected becomes shaky. It no longer supports the settlers' claims to exclusive enjoyment.

The events at Cronulla on 11 December 2005 were a protest and a stand against this unravelling. Subsequent reports in the media portrayed the locals' acts of violence as those of a besieged and dispossessed people. The dispossession experienced by others does not rate a mention. This is a local order that is simultaneously national, an order that suppresses the diversity of who can be a local, and truly Australian. Yet surely the Cronulla Riot and its aftermath, during which the idea of multiculturalism has come into question, will not be the last word. The tension between being an Australian citizen – equal under the law with other citizens – and being a born-and-bred Australian continues. Increasingly, the phrase 'all Australians' is persistently and defiantly diverse in character, despite being used as a homogenising tool for assimilation. As such, the Australian language of settlement groans as it struggles to hold together individuals as equals while the locals attempt to maintain preeminence in the management of local and national places.

Part Three

WORKING WITH THE NECESSARY OTHER

Chapter Seven

THE CLOSING OF PUBLIC CULTURE
TO COMMUNAL DIFFERENCE

As it's configured within the environment of those parameters, the public sphere is seen as almost the only sphere that's legitimate and we can only come to the public sphere as single individuals and citizens, not as any other kind of category.

Interview with Ashis Nandy, 6 December 2007

Public culture is composed of diverse elements – parliamentary committees, law courts, the media, and the unruly public sphere itself. These varied components are connected by discourses and practices that reach across specific institutions and spaces. Each of our case studies has examined an episode that places questions about the relationship between race and Australian citizenship to the fore of public discourse. The debate about the belonging of non-Anglo Australians occurred, more often than not, in cultural rather than biological terms. Considering how matters of race are reinscribed as questions of culture, in this chapter we examine the relationship between communal traditions, Enlightenment principles and the capacity to dissent. At the time of each case study, there was an opportunity for diverse cultural traditions to be legitimised as presences in the Australian public culture and the nation. And at each moment, Australian public life failed to make room for different communal, cultural traditions. These case studies – or moments – then, are examples of how 'the concept of Enlightenment […] has failed whenever confronted by the concrete reality of difference (exemplified nowadays by the presence of the Indigenous Australian, by the African migrant, the refugees, and their like).'[1] Understanding why this occurred in these case studies can help us to envisage how similar future events might proceed and, hopefully, conclude differently.

In order to examine the limits and effects of Enlightenment public culture, we will be turning to Ashis Nandy's analyses of the relationships between Enlightenment principles, modernity and colonisation in India. Australia's discursive and physical relationship to India is more intimate than might be initially suspected. Like India, Australia is part of Asia and, like India, Australia needs to be understood as a British colony in which British traditions and Enlightenment ideas played out, with attendant effects on non-Anglo cultural traditions present in the colony. The relationship between India and Australia was close at the beginning of the colony. As Stephen Muecke writes,

> In the colonial period, Sydney was strategically placed between India and China (four weeks from [the] Cape of Good Hope, five weeks from Calcutta and China, less than a month from Batavia and two weeks from New Zealand). During the first thirty years of its existence, the Australian colony was visited by over a hundred ships from India alone, starting from 1792. When the first supply ship for the colony the *Guardian* failed to appear, the *Atlantic* was dispatched from Calcutta. The cargo was two hundred and fifty gallons of rum, eight casks flour, eight casks Indian-cured pork, rice, semolina, lentils, samples of ghee, sugar and molasses, seeds and plants, two bulls, two cattle, eight sheep, and twenty goats.[2]

To acknowledge the psychological and physical continuity between the two countries is not to ignore the striking differences between their historical and contemporary circumstances – most notably that, unlike Australia, India is not a settler colony and what is, for a nonsettler colony like India, an 'imperial centre', is for Australia 'the Mother Country.'[3] Nevertheless, the continuities mean that theorising from India is especially useful in developing analyses of certain phenomena in Australia. In particular, India's complex cultural circumstances allow it to exemplify certain issues of culture, power and knowledge tied to the legacy of colonisation. As Nandy points out, 'Contemporary India, by virtue of its bicultural experience, manages to epitomise the global problem of knowledge and power in our times.'[4] He 'throws the spotlight on the colonisers' in India, 'stressing the psychological damage this system did to the British.'[5] In turn, through armies and settlers, this hardened psychology, strengthened in India, was exported to other colonies like Australia and Canada. It has wielded influence in Australia's political culture, which is, as Nandy notes, 'primarily a product of its tendency to see itself as a colonial power – as subaltern colonial power, but a colonial power nonetheless – when it has actually been a colonised society.'[6]

The ideas in Nandy's work that we are focussing on concern the inherent limits that the modern, public culture emerging out of colonial, Enlightenment thought places on the inclusion of colonised and non-European cultural traditions. The first theme we will consider is how scientific, historical and political discourses emerging out of Enlightenment thought come to form the means by which traditional cultural knowledges and values are dismissed in a colonial context. For example, in the context of the promotion of tolerance, it is assumed that an Enlightenment understanding is the only source of tolerance, and that the resources available in other cultural traditions for tolerance and understanding are overlooked and dismissed. The situation is aggravated when Enlightenment discourses are ineffective in promoting tolerance and, indeed, when they play an intrinsic part in the marginalisation of different cultural practices and understandings. As we saw in Chapter Two, one source of this dismissal of traditional cultural knowledges lies in the inherent inability of the Enlightenment principles that took hold in Australia to acknowledge the role and value of communal traditions and membership of different cultural groups.

A second theme of Nandy's to emerge, particularly from the *Cubillo* case, is how the demands of modern national history serve to dismiss the value of communal membership and experience. As such, it is one way in which the significance of communal membership is removed in favour of an unmediated relationship between individuals and the state. The difficulties that affect the representation of diverse cultural groups are a result both of how the ways in which history is practised serve to marginalise certain kinds of experience, and also of how the idea of modern history itself works against non-European cultures. In removing the importance of communal membership, national history limits the possibilities for legitimate dissent, and renders inaudible the voices of those experiencing suffering due to communal membership. By eliminating critical voices, such practices also limit the accountability of the nation.

Finally, Nandy's work on the 'psychology of exile' and the experience of the transition to secular modernity of traditional cultural groups allows us to think about how the experience of uprootedness in this shift is as relevant to Australian British settler communities as it is to other migrant communities. Importantly, Nandy highlights how the experiences of uprooting and exile do not only affect the transnational immigrant, but also those who culturally migrate within a nation, including movements from the country to the city, and between classes, eras and cultures.

The 1858 Bill: Traditions of Tolerance and Exclusions of Enlightenment

During the 1858 inquiry, some participants and commentators supportive of Chinese immigration called, not on universally valid ideas in accordance with Enlightenment thinking, but on British religious and traditional values. The *Sydney Morning Herald* warned against the adoption of the proposed law, noting that the legislators, 'upon the very first appearance of a people whom it is possible to oppress, heap upon them the fiercest calumnies,' and 'insult and assault them […] in a crusade so disgraceful to our Christian civilisation.'[7] Robert Isaacs's speech in the Legislative Council itself invoked the 'wisdom of the ancients', the 'well springs of Christianity', the 'confidence in the physique and morale of Britons', the 'vitality in the Anglo-Saxon institutions' and the 'mighty river of Christianity.'[8] While Isaacs problematically asserted that Britons are a superior race due to their birth and breeding, this superiority was rationalised not in terms of science, progress and the social contract, but in terms of the religious and institutional traditions of which Isaacs was so confident. This open calling on British religious and cultural traditions is worth exploring for several reasons.

Firstly, it demonstrates a significant contrast with the Indian experience of the importation of Enlightenment political thought. Nandy notes that, in India, these ideas were largely introduced in abstract form via texts and concepts, not as part of a lived tradition with a cultural context.[9] In the comments of Isaacs and the *Sydney Morning Herald*, however, we see a continuity with a lived tradition of British politics that is called on as the basis for examining the question of Chinese immigration. Further, we can note that this British cultural tradition is serving as a basis on which to justify the acceptance of Chinese immigration – Isaacs's confidence in British tradition seems to be the basis of his lack of fear, and thus tolerance, of Chinese immigrants. Likewise, the *Sydney Morning Herald*'s reference to Christianity and Anglo-Saxon institutions saw them as a foundation for tolerance of Chinese immigrants. Perhaps surprisingly, then, the appeal to British cultural traditions and religions, however much the notion of a unified British culture is itself an effect of colonisation, can be related to the tolerance of non-Anglo immigrants.

While tolerance might be thought by some to be the prerogative of Enlightenment political frameworks, Nandy makes the point that different cultural traditions can also provide frameworks for tolerance, suggesting that we can look for principles of tolerance within religious and cultural traditions.[10] Such grounds for tolerance leads to the acceptance of the existence of multiple groups' values and traditions even if there is hostility between groups – for, as Nandy writes, 'distances and hostilities, like closeness and friendship, have specific, culturally defined meanings.'[11] These various forms of tolerance drawn from diverse traditions can be the source of a tolerance of all for all, rather than the tolerance of a dominant group for all others.[12] In the context of the inquiry, this would be a form of tolerance specific to British cultures and traditions.

The dynamics of the inquiry further raise the question of whether the principles within British cultural traditions were potentially more effective than the Enlightenment framework for tolerance. In contrast to Isaacs and the *Sydney Morning Herald* article, a number of participants in the inquiry most concerned about the presence of the Chinese drew on aspects of Enlightenment thinking in a complex manner. These ideas were central to the persistence of apprehension about the Chinese, despite the evidence that they were model citizens. Anxiety remained about Chinese immigration because, although their behaviour was good, the cultural traditions and values underlying this behaviour were not thought to be acceptable.

Those concerned about Chinese immigration pursued discourses of population management relating to hygiene, sexuality and gender in an attempt to demonstrate that the Chinese were a potential threat to the Anglo-Australian population. Committee members took up matters of disease and hygiene regardless of evidence that the Chinese were remarkably clean given the conditions they were often forced to live in. Possibilities of miscegenation and homosexuality were raised, with little concern for the contradiction between allegations that the Chinese men were a threat both because they were homosexual and because they were marrying Anglo-Saxon women. The deployment of such discourses during colonisation is well known.[13] In particular, the repeated characterisation of British subjects as adult, male and securely heterosexual – in contrast to the childlike, feminine and possibly homosexual colonised – has been noted by Nandy, who points out that 'colonialism reactivated the fear of liminality which women and children invoked in the European culture by being at the margin between human beings and nature.'[14]

In the mid-nineteenth century, roughly the time of the inquiry, the theory of imperialism began to take shape, drawing on modern technology as a justification for colonisation and the basis of the superiority of Western culture over superstitious savages.[15] The hierarchy between European and non-European civilisations 'crystallised out as a by-product of the Enlightenment [...] [and] was neatly picked up by Western colonialism and science.'[16] Thus we see medical discourse relating to population management at the forefront of racialising of issues of national health through the targeting of Chinese immigrants for small pox vaccination. While the Chinese were not – in the context of the inquiry – the colonised, but rather a non-Anglo culture merely seeking a presence in a colonial country, the hierarchies between civilisations stimulated and deployed by colonialism came into play. And like their deployment against colonised people, the 'hierarchical principles deriving from age and sex, already prominent in European cosmology, were combined with this justification to forge a composite picture of the coloniser – scientific, technologically skilled, bearing the responsibility of history and dutifully playing a civilising role.'[17]

It was not easy to characterise the Chinese immigrants in an entirely negative manner. In New South Wales, Chinese residents were maintaining their traditions and successfully surviving in the face of hardship, poverty and cultural dominance. Yet the grudging admittance during the inquiry that the Chinese were virtuous considered this to be despite their cultural traditions, rather than a result of them. Their virtue could be accepted only if it was justified in the terms of the concerned Anglo-Australian committee members. Requiring that the Chinese justify their behaviour in terms of a colonial worldview and the human sciences of the time allowed the British to dismiss their behaviour as unwanted. That which was not expressed in the terms of scientific discourse was excluded. It is an instance, in Nandy's words, of 'the operationalism which reduces reality to the reality accessible to the methods of science, and then reconstructs the "whole" reality – of nature, of persons or cultures – by extrapolating from that operational reality.'[18] And it was precisely the success of the Chinese that necessitated this reduction. The Chinese were a confusion and a threat to the colonial framework of a hierarchy of civilisations. In such a context, their good behaviour, rather than leading to acceptance, was a potential disruption to the worldview of many Anglo-Australians. The need to firmly contain Chinese cultures was pressing, lest it upset the justification for colonialism's civilising endeavour.

This civilising mission was a unifying aim across the colonies, and the fear of the Chinese immigrants occurred in a transnational context. J. V. D'Cruz has written of how the events concerning the Chinese in 1858 occurred in the context of another colonial event – the Indian Mutiny. In April of that year, words and money were contributed in support of the Indian Mutiny Relief Fund on the basis of, as stated in the NSW Parliament (the same parliament in which the Chinese inquiry was being conducted),

> [...] the incalculable importance of our Indian possessions [...] as, humanely speaking, the only means of raising nearly two hundred millions of men from a brutish, and also hopeless degradation; a condition which seems to unite the evils of an effete civilisation with those of unreclaimed barbarism; of a subtle and intellectual refinement with utter absence of moral restraint, or spiritual aspirations.[19]

A colonial psychology closely linked India and Australia at this point, and the fear of the Indian Mutiny was intimately entangled with questions of race and civilisation within Australia. Indeed, D'Cruz concludes that, 'the Chinese became vaguely an immediate miniature of the enemy in far off India.'[20]

The 1858 bill to restrict Chinese immigration to NSW was rejected, but not before it established categories, terms and hierarchical structures that persisted in debates about the legitimacy of non-Anglo Australian citizens. We can see in the inquiry the use of discourses regarding medicine and population management to discredit a non-Anglo-Saxon cultural tradition and to exclude people of Chinese background from Australian citizenship. But it is worth noting that the contributions to and the comments on the inquiry included both reference to British culture as well as Enlightenment principles and associated human sciences that had gained a hold in Australia. Indeed, as noted previously, many of those strongly opposed to the bill called with confidence on British cultural traditions as grounds for accepting the Chinese. Although there was no acceptance of Chinese cultural traditions as a justification for their behaviour and values, Anglo-Australian participants in and commentators on the inquiry were not obliged to disown their affiliation with British cultural and religious traditions. There was no overwhelming demand that the inquiry appear culturally neutral, and thus no demand that the Enlightenment thinking associated with New South Wales parliamentary practice deny its relationship to British traditions and single handedly determine the terms and categories of the debate.

Cubillo v. the Commonwealth (2000): History, Civilisation and Accountability

The oscillation during the 1858 inquiry between calling simultaneously on a British cultural tradition strong enough to withstand the presence of Chinese culture and on discourses of disease, hygiene and sexuality related to Enlightenment frameworks of knowledge to justify the exclusion of the Chinese stands in strong contrast to the more strictly regulated discourse of the second case study – the *Cubillo* case. In this second case study, the place for cultural traditions in public culture was more strictly controlled, and not only were non-Anglo cultural values and traditions marginalised (in this case, Indigenous cultural values and traditions), the role that Anglo-cultural values and traditions played was also veiled (although not necessarily absent). According to the principles of universality and impartiality governing the courts, it is imperative that no cultural bias is overtly displayed in the conduct of cases, particularly ones as politically relevant and scrutinised as *Cubillo*. Part of the British common law tradition is that the law is seen as a culturally neutral arbitrator, which requires that neither Anglo-Australian cultural traditions nor Indigenous cultural traditions should be seen to bias proceedings. But the Australian legal practice arising from the tradition of British common law retains a problematic cultural partiality. The conduct of the *Cubillo* case displayed this bias in the conceptual edifice within which it was conducted, which restricted the court's ability to adequately adjudicate such a culturally complex case. The particular aspects of this bias that we are interested in are those that suppressed the relevance of membership of a traditional communal group to the examination of the events under investigation. The practice and concept of history in the court was an especially important element in this process.

While Lorna Cubillo and Peter Gunner brought their cases as individual citizens to the Federal Court, their claims for damages were based on the Commonwealth's actions 'under the dictate of' a general policy of removing 'half-caste' children without regard to their individual circumstances. The question of the relevance of the children's membership of a racial group and its effects on their individual treatment was thus crucial to the case. Accordingly, arguing against the relevance of their membership of a racial group was important for the Commonwealth's defence. There was, the Commonwealth argued and established, no such general policy of removing 'half-caste children' in the Northern Territory in the 1950s, so the claimants' membership of a racially identified group was deemed immaterial. Further, the court established that the children were removed as individuals with, in Peter Gunner's instance, parental consent and, in Lorna Cubillo's, effectively parental consent. Establishing that the children were not removed because of their membership of a racial group *prima facie* dismissed the role that membership of a communal group played in the forced removals. The court case became a question of the individual's unmediated relationship to the law.

Establishing this unmediated relationship between the individual and the law supports, of course, the urgent need to see the court as culturally neutral. All individuals are equal before the law, and whether an individual is Anglo-Australian or Indigenous Australian must appear irrelevant to the court's proceedings. But, we argue, the removal of questions of the impact and role of communal membership on the legal proceedings is, by default, to privilege those within the Anglo-Australian cultural tradition underlying Australian legal institutions and discourses.

In particular, the European understanding of history used in the court's proceedings crucially controlled the version of events accepted by the court and was a key contributor in dismissing the impact that membership of different cultural groups might have had on past and present events. As discussed in the case study, the proof accepted by the court for establishing historical events was documentary evidence. In effect, what it admitted as documentary evidence was considered the historical facts.[21] The court's distinction between the historical 'facts' of a case as established by documentary evidence, and historical accounts established through research and analysis, worked against the plaintiffs. The former was acceptable; the latter was regarded with scepticism. Ann McGrath was cross-examined for five days, and Peter Read subsequently decided not to offer his report to the court. There was a dearth of documentary evidence surrounding the removal of the children. The documents that did exist, such as that containing the thumbprint of Peter Gunner's mother – supposedly indicating consent to his removal – bore extraordinary weight. The suspicion about oral testimony, central to understanding Aboriginal history, also worked against the claimants. This recourse to a strict, empiricist account of history comes close to simply conflating it with the empiricist practices of law.

This assumption, and the court's restricted view of history, supported a bias towards Anglo-Australian cultural standards in the court that is inherent in the concept of history itself. Reflecting on the relationship between history and colonialism, Nandy writes of history's

> […] civilisational hubris that claims that not merely the present but even the past and the future of some cultures have to be reworked. The main tools in that redefinition till now have been devaluation, marginalisation, and liquidation of memories that cannot be historicised and, in the case of cultures that locate their utopias in their past, narrowing the range of alternatives 'envisionable' within the cultures.[22]

His point here is that history is only one means of understanding the past, a means that was integral to the conceptual framework surrounding European colonial dominance. Inherent in the concept of history is the idea that history is the sole means by which the past should be understood. The possibility of other valid relationships to the past, such as mythologisation, is rejected. This understanding of history 'cannot accept that history can be dealt with from outside history; the entire Enlightenment worldview militates against such a proposition.'[23] Ahistorical understandings of the past are perceived to be savage or primitive, for, in Nandy's words, '"the historians'"" history of the ahistorical – when grounded in a "proper" historical consciousness, as defined by the European Enlightenment – is usually a history of the prehistorical, the primitive, and the pre-scientific.'[24] The idea of history is thus complicit in the establishment and maintenance of the hierarchy between civilisations – or the 'civilised' and the 'non-civilised' – that provided the initial justification for colonialism's dispossession of Indigenous peoples and its civilising endeavours. Civilised people *have* history and, *within* history the 'primitive' needs to be trained and educated to become 'civilised.' There is no 'outside' to history in which nonmodern peoples can reside.

The civilising process occurring within history is one in which groups with different, nonmodern cultural traditions over time become part of a universal, modern community. History leads inevitably to modernity, and in this way it carries with it a devaluing of membership of differing communal traditions, which are seen as something to be eventually done away with. In Australia, this took the form of the view that Indigenous Australians would inevitably be assimilated into European culture. In the context of South Asia, Nandy writes of

> [...] the presumption that societies, like biological species, move from a more primitive stage encoded in traditions, towards a modern, secular humanism that de-ethnicises all communities. For such evolutionism, communalism defines an earlier stage of development and is a throw back to such a stage, and the prognosis is that, with the forces of secular individualism gaining ground, communalism in South Asia will die a predictable death.[25]

We see here how the imperative to view cultural traditions as merely stages of development allows for their dismissal, and is connected to the demand for an unmediated relationship between the individual and the state. This view underlies the difficulty courts have in recognising the role cultural-group membership plays in events, even when it seems so essential to understanding them. This configuration of ideas, then, is part of the modern Australian court in which the cases of Cubillo and Gunner were conducted, and it contributed to rendering communal membership irrelevant to their claims against the Commonwealth.

   But the absence of a role for membership of culturally different groups in the courtroom existed only superficially. It was a response to the demand, particularly urgent in this instance, that the institutions of public life are culturally neutral in an increasingly multicultural society. At a number of points in the conduct of the case, it became very difficult to conceal the role that cultural norms were playing, especially in the idea that proof was required that those removing the children acted with inappropriate motives according to the law and community 'standards of the time'. The court focussed on a single set of dominant Anglo-Australian standards, ruling out the possibility that the values and standards of multiple cultural groups were relevant to evaluating the circumstances and the effect of an Indigenous child's removal. But in the effort to see the court as objective, neither Anglo-Australian communal values nor Indigenous ones could be seen to have a place. To raise the question of multiple communal traditions would be to invoke the spectre of just what role British communal values are playing in the courtroom. The requirement that the case be seen as a culturally impartial adjudication, an issue between the neutral court and the individuals, means that the question of whether there were relevant Indigenous cultural traditions could not be duly considered. To do so in such a context questions the validity of the modern courtroom and the conceptual edifice supporting it, undermining its authority.

In the call on history to 'provide the historical facts' by which the case was to be adjudicated, we see a powerful instance of how the very terms and categories of the court were those of an Enlightenment worldview that was not culturally neutral, but predisposed towards Anglo-Australian culture. The Indigenous claimants were required to justify themselves in the terms and categories of those who allegedly mistreated them. This circumstance is not unique to cases relating to the Australian state's removal of Indigenous children, or, indeed, to Australia.[26] It is an all-too-frequent consequence of the colonisation of non-European lands and peoples by European people and ideas. While colonisation has ceased and reparation for past wrongs can be sought, the victims' claims are to be heard in a forum driven by the legacy of European ideas and frameworks of value. In *Culture, Voice and Development*, Nandy writes:

> One characteristic of the Enlightenment worldview underpinning modernity is the stipulation that all dissent from modernity, to qualify as worthwhile, must be expressed in a language consistent with modernity, particularly with the demands of historical consciousness, the theory of progress, and scientific rationality.[27]

In the context of the *Cubillo* case, we can see this understanding of dissent in the court's demand that it disputed the legitimacy of their removal by using a conceptual framework that is incompatible with the valuing of Indigenous groups' cultural traditions, and that validates those of colonialism. Nandy considers such constraints on dissent as pathological and one of the most serious objections to the modernist project.[28] It serves to suppress dissent that is not couched in modernity's terms, rendering it 'inaudible.'[29]

Modernity's restriction of dissent to its own terms in this manner intensely reduces the capacity of the Australian public culture to accept responsibility and be accountable for the suffering caused by actions justified in Enlightenment terms. Yet this capacity, according to Nandy, is an essential component of the evaluation of any vision of and for the world. Ziauddin Sardar writes:

> Future utopias and visions, Nandy contends, must have an in-built ability to account for their legitimate and illegitimate offspring. The oppressive actions of zealous visionaries in the name of their visions cannot be simply explained away as the actions of misguided adherents or products of misuse or deviations or false interpretations. A vision must take the responsibility of what is undertaken in its name. What this means is that the vision itself must have some capacity to liberate the visionaries from its own straightjacket.[30]

This view contrasts strikingly with the commonly expressed opinion, often presented as an exoneration, that the suffering of removed children was the result of good but misguided intentions. Judge O'Loughlin thought this point needed making in his conclusion, which states that the people who removed Aboriginal children 'thought of themselves as well meaning and well intentioned but who today would be characterised by many as badly misguided bureaucrats. Those people thought that they were acting in the best interests of the child.'[31] The important point that Nandy is making about the need for visions for the world to be accountable relates to the capacity of adherents to these worldviews to accept responsibility for what is done in their name, and to acknowledge and examine what *within* them has generated suffering and injustice. The conduct of the *Cubillo* case suggests that, in key components of Australian public life, such as the courts – where reparations can be sought – the limits and injustices of Enlightenment principles unfortunately persist. If the Enlightenment's vision, as later manifest in the *Cubillo* case, is 'judged not so much by what is done in its name as by its ability to sanctify accountability and self-exploration', then it disappoints.[32]

In the *Cubillo* case, we see the flourishing of Enlightenment principles and the suppression of their relationship to British traditions, at the same moment as Indigenous communal values are dismissed. At the moment of this court case, the values of progress, impartiality and universality are presented as independent of any tradition, and the supporting role of Anglo cultural traditions covered by a somewhat ineffective sleight of hand. Confidence in British culture and tradition is not openly expressed. Indeed, even though the notion of 'standards of the time' was used to defend the removal and detention of the children, there was no attempt to defend these standards – they too were seen as just another misguided way-station on route to modernity.

The Cronulla Riot (2005): The Psychology of Exile

The dissociation of Enlightenment principles from the British traditions that supported their establishment and maintenance is an inherent part of any project that claims universality and neutrality. But, as noted in our discussion of the 1858 inquiry, the compulsion to perform such a distancing has not always been as strongly present in Australian public institutions as it was during the *Cubillo* case. This distancing becomes imperative in contemporary Australia because of the need for public institutions to appear objective in the face of an increasing presence of non-British traditions within the nation. With the rise in post–World War II immigration and the obvious need to acknowledge Indigenous Australians' presence both prior to and within the nation, it was pressing that public culture began to appear more culturally objective. As discussed in Chapter Two, the Enlightenment tradition that took hold in Australia was a particularly instrumental and utilitarian one, rendering it ready to distance public culture from its association with British tradition when practical.

Yet this distancing may not always be well received by those who consider themselves part of the Anglo-Australian tradition, and this, we suggest, is one of the ingredients contributing to the intensities surrounding the Cronulla Riot. During the riot, we saw Cronulla 'locals' protesting against and attacking visitors from the western suburbs, perceived by the locals to be Arab, Middle Eastern and/or Muslim. Although these latter groups are not congruent, they were frequently perceived to be so in the heady climate after the September 11 attacks.[33] The beach is a key space of Australian public culture, to which its constructions of national identity have increasingly appealed.[34] Baden Offord has noted that, 'As the site of European invasion, of the first encounter between minds that were separated by thousands of years of knowledge, experience and being, the beach in Australia is a powerful symbol of civilisation, its creation and destruction.'[35]

The Cronulla Riot physically played out the struggle over just which culture legitimately belongs in Australian public space, as well as which values should inform it. According to the protestors and rioters, the beach was actually the property of 'locals' who were 'born and bred' in Cronulla. These locals openly supported Anglo-Australian cultural traditions, and considered the visitors' behaviour as in conflict with Anglo-Australian standards and values. As Amelia Johns notes of her interviews about the riot with Anglo-Australians in Cronulla in 2006 and 2007, 'themes of Christianity, nationalism and white Australian rules seem to have become fused together, forming a homologous set of cultural traditions against which Muslims and Lebanese are cast as un-Australian.'[36] The Cronulla Riot expressed and generated the well-examined fear that Anglo-Australian culture in the nation might be overwhelmed by the (supposedly inferior) cultural traditions of non-European immigrants. This fear was intensified by the idea that Anglo-Australian culture did not enjoy the same levels of support from the state as it once had.

According to such a modern state, where one was born, or the communal traditions one has inherited, are irrelevant to a sense of belonging once one has acquired citizenship. The first-generation immigrant belongs no less than the fourth-, and the alliance between the state and British tradition is downplayed. The Cronulla Riot was partly driven by a fear of the weakening of the alliance between the instrumental and multicultural modern state of Australia and Anglo-Australian cultures. The Howard government's maintenance of high immigration levels while simultaneously symbolically accentuating that Australia's core values and culture should be in the British tradition surely created greater confusion for groups experiencing anxiety over this matter.

The Cronulla Riot presents a white Australian masculinity – one that was formerly accentuated and hardened through the experience of colonialism – as being in peril. Gender was central to the riot, with the Anglo-Australian rioters claiming that Muslim visitors to the beach were introducing the mistreatment of women into the country. Australian women and Australian values apparently needed protection against such treatment. This threat to women calls into question the masculinity of their protectors. The idea of a white masculinity under threat was in broad circulation at the time of the riot. As Katherine Bode writes,

> One of the images that became definitive of the Cronulla race riots – of a young man, draped in an Australian flag with the slogan, 'We grew here, you flew here', painted on his body – signifies a particularly blatant symbol of this juxtaposition of whiteness, masculinity, self-proclaimed suffering and nationalism. The credence given to the idea that the rights of white Australian men have been overwhelmed by the claims of women and other races disrupts the dominant battle narrative underlying and enabling hegemonic constructions of white Australian masculinity. In this context it is possible that the trope of male damage prevalent in the Australian media and culture offers a more reliable way of upholding white male power and privilege.[37]

The interviews by Johns suggest that the riot was at least partly a display of 'macho-ness' on both sides. In this sense, resemblance and competition between Anglo-Australian masculinity and the masculinity of the visitors to the beach motivated the violence of the riot, because the latter was perceived as a threat to the former.[38] This notion of white masculinity under threat paradoxically serves to reinforce the idea that white males (of Anglo heritage) have a traditional right over the Australian land. The fear that Anglo-Australians will be exiled from Australia assumes the primacy of an Anglo-Australian cultural tradition in Australia that needs to be protected.

Nandy's work on the psychology of uprooted cultures and the experiences of exile can further help us understand the dynamics of the fear underlying the riot. His understanding of those who lose touch with communal, cultural traditions is not restricted to those who experience the effects of migrating between nation states. The experience of unrootedness can also occur *within* the nation, as people transition from traditional cultures to secular modernity. On the one hand, he observes, many aspects of secular, modern values have a deep attraction for people who have been distanced, literally and psychologically, from communal traditions.[39] According to modernity's understanding of the unmediated relationship between individual and state, nothing of value need be lost in the transition away from traditional values. One's membership of a communal tradition or place of birth is not relevant in any substantial way once one is a citizen of the nation state. Communal cultural and religious traditions can be maintained in the private sphere, but have no role in the public, so citizens need not fear that their traditions will adversely affect their treatment in that realm.

On the other hand, the dominance of a supposedly culturally neutral, secular framework of values also generates anger and defensiveness on behalf of those who fear the loss of their communal traditions. Nandy writes:

> [...] massive uprooting has produced a cultural psychology of exile that in turn has led to an unending search for roots, on the one hand, and angry, sometimes self-destructive, assertion of nationality and ethnicity on the other. As the connection with the past has weakened, desperate attempts to re-establish this connection have also grown.[40]

In the context of the Cronulla Riot, our point is not that this fear was manifest in the visitors to the beach – those perceived to be immigrants and foreigners (noting, of course, that a number of these visitors were born in Australia) – but that it was present in those claiming to be 'locals': those afraid that, with the rise of globalisation and the modern multicultural state, their Anglo-Australian culture would be lost. As Nandy's analyses of the rise of Hindutva in India demonstrates, the anxiety experienced by those who fear the loss of their culture is not necessarily most intensely experienced by cultural minorities within a nation; it also preoccupies culturally dominant groups.[41] Such fear renders people particularly vulnerable to manipulation by political parties, Indian or Australian, making it an especially important cultural phenomenon to examine.

Conclusion

The three case studies we have discussed are ones in which issues of race and culture are central. Often, the justification for the mistreatment or exclusion of non-Anglo Australians is put in terms of an inferior and morally or practically problematic culture.[42] The justification of mistreatment on cultural grounds is frequently covertly present in the mechanisms and standards of the tradition of Australian public culture. In contemporary times, this clandestine bias is due to the political demand that the public sphere and its culture be neutral, treating different communal traditions even handedly. The idea of the possibility of a culturally neutral public sphere is a legacy of the Australian Enlightenment tradition, but it is precisely this desire to see public life as culturally neutral – and the failure to openly acknowledge and address its partiality – that limits public culture's engagement with non-European cultural traditions. We suggest that doing away with the idea that sites and discourses of public life can be culturally impartial – some kind of space universally equally accessible to all – needs to be part of rendering that space a genuinely multicultural and racially equal forum.

To acknowledge the legitimate presence of cultures in the public sphere, and their positive and negative effects, is to dispute the very terms and conditions of modern public culture. The claim that communal, cultural traditions are and should remain alive in public life (in contrast to private life) conflicts with the understanding that such traditions are a stage of development, a stage that will be ultimately overcome by rational interrogation in the public sphere. It is in this sense that, according to Nandy, the idea of culture itself is a form of resistance to the terms and categories of a unified modern world, rejecting the 'stipulation and the assumption that the future shape of all human consciousness was decided once and for all in seventeenth-century Europe.'[43]

The Enlightenment tradition of the public sphere and its associated institutions and culture allows for the libratory practice of challenging and dismissing traditional authorities through public, critical debate. The accomplishments of this tradition are not to be viewed lightly, but the limitations it places on dissent need to be recognised. Nandy writes that we must realise that 'yesterday's dissent is often today's establishment and, unless resisted, becomes tomorrow's terror.'[44] This thought applies to the principles shaping Australian public culture (as they might one day apply to the idea of culture as dissent), and thus, we suggest, need to be questioned. This is not to reject the tradition of Australian public culture, but to acknowledge that it is a particular cultural tradition rather than universally accessible; a tradition that requires change and renewal. The capacity of a tradition to identify its limits, rather than its universality, is an asset, according to Nandy. A tradition can be recommended by its 'capacity for self-renewal through heterodoxy, plurality and dissent. […] [and in being] open-ended, self-analytic and self-aware without being overly self-conscious.'[45] To encourage these kinds of characteristics in the Australian public culture would be to recreate it as a space with negotiable rather than universal principles, thus allowing for a more genuine dialogue between parties from different communal traditions.[46] Rather than having modernity as their destination and future, communal traditions would be accepted on their terms and conditions. And the presence of communal traditions different from one's own would be tolerated as a necessary aspect of the social fabric, and of the fabric of the sites, institutions and practices of our public life.

This view of the place of non-Anglo Australian cultural traditions and, concurrently, Anglo-Australian cultural traditions calls upon the idea that the existence of unfamiliar cultures and traditions is unavoidable and a welcome way for, in this case, Anglo-Australians to define themselves. This attitude towards a different cultural group can be described as the idea of 'the necessary other', according to which one sees others as an unavoidable part of oneself, because identity is inevitably developed in relationship with others. This, we think, is what Nandy is pointing towards when he writes, 'one has to relive one's self-definition as much through one's enemies as through one's friends. [...] one needs one's enemies to define oneself and one is aware every moment that one is incomplete without them.'[47] Whether friend or enemy, mutual dependence means that the existence of necessary others and their unfamiliar cultural traditions is acknowledged as legitimate. This kind of self-understanding recognises that the self cannot be disentangled from its others in its process of self-definition. As Nandy points out, in not seeking to be a pure identity independent of others, such self-definition works against the desire to eliminate or repress others in our understandings of the past, present and future.[48] To understand that one exists only in the context of others generates resistance to the idea that there is a single, common story or history by which we understand ourselves. Different people have varying means of self-definition and self-understanding, and these are interrelated and interdependent. The legitimacy of the existence of multiple groups' values and traditions is accepted, even if there is some hostility between groups.[49] The dynamics of this kind of interrelationship between cultural groups should be allowed into and, most importantly, should fundamentally shape Australian public life.

To accept the idea that communal traditions have no role in negotiating the standards and practices of public life is to accept the view that cultures and their traditions are only a stop on the road to an already established form of modernity – a modernity in which the individual exists in an unmediated relationship with the state and its institutions. But if, as D'Cruz observes of his own experience, the negotiation of a secure place of belonging arises not out of the rejection of 'little cultures' but from within them,[50] then diverse cultural traditions should not be written out of the nation. Or perhaps, more accurately, they cannot be written out because, in Nandy's words, 'cultures are refusing to sing their swansongs and bow out of the world stage to enter the textbooks of history. Indeed, cultures have now begun to return, like Freud's unconscious, to haunt the modern system of nation states.'[51] We think this return can be welcomed.

Afterword

THE EMPTINESS WITHIN AND WITHOUT: ENLIGHTENMENT AUSTRALIA AND ITS DEMONS

Vinay Lal

'Happy families are all alike', says the famous line with which Tolstoy commenced his novel *Anna Karenina*, and 'every unhappy family is unhappy in its own way'. I suspect that as much is true of nations: all happy nations, in the conventional wisdom, are happy in much the same way, largely attentive to the minimal material needs of their subjects, protective of those rights to freedom of speech, mobility and religious worship which may be considered as fundamental to notions of human liberty and dignity, and energized by a citizenry that is not merely well-fed but at least in principle invested in the idea that, in the words of Mohandas Gandhi, 'the good of the individual is contained in the good of the all.'[1] And, yet, if Tolstoy may be stretched some, nations appear to be unhappy also for very much similar reasons, afflicted by familiar problems of racism, sexual discrimination and class inequality, myopically protective of what is termed national self-interest, often wary of the stranger, or besotted by those myriad social ailments that the ingenuity of man has created.

Nevertheless, it may be that each nation has to confront demons that are particularly its own, which may be one way of describing the subject matter of *Inside Australian Culture: Legacies of Enlightenment Values*. Every word in this title, as the authors are all too aware, invites discussion, interrogation, even disagreement. How does one, for instance, get inside a nation? If there is ever getting inside a nation, is it only to discover that, as Ernest Renan put it, forgetting is just as important to building a nation as remembering?[2] Is the presence of the 'other' the very condition of being forged into a nation, and in what respects is this true of Australia? What a nation chooses to suppress about itself is perhaps more revealing than what it celebrates, commemorates and canonizes. Who all claim, and with what degree of legitimacy, to be speaking as Australians and who are all occluded when 'enlightenment values' are summoned to establish and authorize hierarchies?

Suppose that one were to construct (following Roland Barthes) an empire of signs around Australia. In place of ramen, Satori, Kabuki, Zen, and pachinko,[3] would we substitute Foster's, Bondi Beach, Ayers Rock, Australian rules and the kangaroo? If we did, *whose* Australia would we have invoked? To whom does Australia belong? When we ask to whom it belongs, have we not already signified our accession to the idea of private property and the ideology of what came to be known as the Enlightenment? Ironically, at no other time was the idea of the savage 'other' invested with such ontological primacy as it was during the Enlightenment, when the idea of the 'natural rights of man' was born. Even as Voltaire was displaying a keen interest in the civilization of China, Eastern Europe – more than anything else, the land, in the view of the great Enlightenment figures, of the semi-human Slavs – was providing Western Europe with a model close to home of 'underdevelopment.'[4] The Enlightenment never bequeathed documents of civilization alone, but of barbarism as well.[5]

Many scholars have been tempted to treat Australia as among one of a group of settler societies that, in a period of some 250 to 300 years after Columbus set foot in the Americas, came to mark the outposts of European civilization. Everywhere the encounter with the white man was calamitous for the indigenous people, leading to genocide, the heartless deployment of a machinery of extermination, the obliteration of entire cultures and lifestyles, the transformation of landscapes and, though this has taken much longer to recognize, the substitution of the knowledge systems of the West for indigenous forms of knowledge. To be sure, the precise manner in which white Europeans made their presence felt may not always have been the same, even if European settlement always sounded the death knell for indigenous peoples. Settlement patterns across the colonies, for example, displayed differences: thus, even though the injunction to 'go west' was followed in Australia and the United States alike, in Australia the white population would be overwhelmingly confined, as is still the case today, to the coastline and its proximity. The great midwest of the United States, pivoting around the metropolis of Chicago, has no counterpart in Australia; on the other hand, the 'bush' and 'outback' still resonate strongly in Australian life, suggesting, if ever so faintly, the risks and thrills of momentary withdrawal from 'civilization.'

In this vein one might go on describing the manner in which Australia is similar to, and different from, the United States or other settler colonies. Though the political leaders of the United States and Great Britain speak of a 'special relationship' between their two countries, seemingly epitomized in comparatively recent times by the close bond that developed between Ronald Reagan and Margaret Thatcher, and then sealed by Tony Blair's unstinting support to George Bush in his aggressive merchandising and execution of a 'war on terror', the notion that the United States is tied to Britain by some umbilical cord ceased to have much traction in American society a long time ago. Australia, on the other hand, has had a more difficult time disentangling itself from the mother country, though this is signified by much more than the presence of the Union Jack within Australia's national flag or the fact that at the apex of the parliamentary system of the Commonwealth of Australia is the British monarch. It is striking that no sooner was Federation accomplished in 1901 that the 'White Australia' policy at once became the law of the land. Indeed, Federation itself rode on the back of the idea that, as the New South Wales Premier Henry Parkes wrote, 'the crimson thread of kinship runs through us all. Even the native-born Australians are Britons, as much as the men born within the cities of London and Glasgow. We know the value of their British origin. We know that we represent a race [...] for the purposes of settling new colonies, which never had its equal on the face of the earth.'[6] Parkes did not live to see Federation, but he would have agreed with the gentleman from the Melbourne Chamber of Commerce who assured a gathering in London that 'we are not a new nation – we don't want to be – but in reality we are only part of a nation [Britain], a large and growing part [... and] desire nothing better than to be part of the great people from whom we have sprung.'[7]

A greater political figure than Parkes suggested just how strong could be the sentiments white Australians experienced when their thoughts turned to Britain. Later to become the longest serving Prime Minister in Australia's history, Robert Menzies penned these thoughts in his diary when his eyes first set sight on Britain in 1935: 'At last we are in England. Our journey to Mecca has ended and our minds abandoned to reflections which can so strangely (unless you remember our traditions and upbringings) move the sense of those who go "home" to a land they have never seen.'[8] 'White Australia' went well beyond being the name of an overtly racist policy: it was the name of a mood, a sentiment, an entire worldview pursued with diligence across all walks of life. The authors of this book revisit, in their chapter on *Cubillo v. the Commonwealth* (2000), one of the more sordid chapters of the 'White Australia' saga captured under the rubric of 'Stolen Generations.' Though the Human Rights and Equal Opportunity Commission advised the Australian Government to recompense those 'half-caste' or part Aboriginal children who had been forcibly separated from their parents, severed from their language, culture and attachment to ancestral lands, more than one court was to pronounce, as our authors argue, the 'destruction of family and cultural links' an unfortunate consequence but

not the purpose of Government policy. In the *Cubillo* case, the judge ruled
that the laws under which half-caste children had been removed, such as the
Aboriginals Ordinance and the Welfare Ordinance, were not to be regarded
as examples of punitive legislation but rather were to be regarded as examples
of 'welfare or caring legislation'. Still, the story of the 'Stolen Generations'
has now come under full public scrutiny[9]; much lesser known are other forms
of 'caring' to which doctors, scientists, eugenicists, anthropologists and a slew
of other professionals were deeply committed in their rigorous quest to secure
a 'White Australia.'[10]

At the heart of Enlightenment Australia, as the five authors of *Inside
Australian Culture* have had the courage to suggest, lurks an ominous emptiness.
On my first visit to Australia in 1983, a reasonably lengthy stay of five months
that took me to Ayers Rock, Coober Pedy, Darwin and Kakadu National Park,
among a great many other places, some in the more remote outback, what
struck me were the immense landscapes and the wide open spaces. It occurred
to me that as many people were born in India every year as peopled the entire
continent of Australia. Thirty years later it remains the same. I recall, almost
as if my experience had transpired the day before yesterday rather than three
decades ago, having the distinct feeling that the great European ambition had
been to 'fill' what were then described to me as 'empty' spaces. There is a
familiar tale, the details of which need not be rehearsed here, of the European
discomfort with these vast 'empty' spaces, but some of its more salient features
may be addressed briefly. The Biblical injunction to multiply and be fruitful did
its bit; the pretense that the land that was about to be occupied was *terra nullius*,
empty land, devoid of inhabitants, would be worked up into a contract that
Europeans gave to themselves as the measure of their eagerness to fulfill God's
command that 'wastelands' should be rendered productive with the labour of
men. There would be variations on this theme: when it became impossible to
deny the Aboriginal presence, white Europeans drew upon the ideas of John
Locke, which had by the eighteenth century become part of Enlightenment
common sense, to advance the argument that the labour of man, and not mere
possession, endowed people with rights to private property. The Aboriginal,
on this reasoning, had not established any rights over property.

What Europeans conceived of as effectively empty land was anything but
empty; indeed, that supposed emptiness without was the emptiness within
the heart of the Enlightenment and its emissaries. Europeans could not see
much less read the tracks that were all too visible to the Aboriginals; they
saw nothing of the songlines in the desert. In the European's encounter with
Aboriginal landscape,[11] which was first imagined as a vast and unproductive
empty space, is to be seen how the notion of place was transformed under
colonial modernity into a generic understanding of space. The Aboriginals

had their own elaborate systems of classification of flora, fauna and foods:[12] rocks, rivers and shrubs were charged with meaning, but the European only saw an inert nature waiting to be transformed by the hand of man.[13] (Much later, some Europeans came to the awareness that Aboriginals had elaborate markings of their landscapes and had an uncanny ability to read traces of humans and animals. Thus would develop the mystique of the tracker,[14] an enigmatic and somewhat unsettling repository of indigenous know-how, the Orientalist obverse of the positivist conception of the Aboriginal as savage.) The colonization of the landscape, fuelled by the 'dream of possession',[15] entailed that each place had to be given a name: as parents name their children, and by so doing take command of them, so the landscape was to be given the characteristics that it had hitherto lacked.[16]

The 'dream of possession', as Offord, Kerruish, Garbutt, Pavlovic and Wessell point out in their discussion of the recent Cronulla Riots, has taken new forms. The 'locals' who strenuously and indeed violently objected to the presence of 'foreigners' and 'bogans' effectively staged two arguments. First, the 'natural' order of Aborigine and white settler was inverted and the settler was installed as the native; secondly, the settler, or in this case what might be called the new Aborigine, was deemed to be 'authentically of a place because of being the first from a place'. Our five authors interestingly invoke Adorno, who deplored 'the barbaric law whereby he who was there first has the greatest rights.'[17] But their intellectual trajectory raises yet another set of questions. Australia was but one place that was sought to be refashioned according to Enlightenment values to fulfil what was presumed to be the only worthwhile idea of a desirable society. In recent years, however, the argument that the Enlightenment was not singular has taken hold among various intellectual constituencies,[18] among them both old-fashioned defenders of the white man's mission as well as, at the other end, postcolonial theorists alarmed at the thought that radical critiques of the Enlightenment might make them vulnerable to charges of being obdurate nativists or third world nationalists. Thus, to take one illustration, Lydia Liu assures us that 'the critique of modernity has always been part of the Enlightenment legacy from the Romantics, Nietzsche, Marx and Heidegger to Horkheimer, Adorno, Foucault, Derrida and even Habermas.'[19] We are enjoined to believe that scholars have become more aware of the 'diversity within the Enlightenment',[20] even that, notwithstanding common impressions of the Enlightenment, many of its savants did not always hold science and religion in opposition to each other.

No one really supposes that the Enlightenment was merely one giant monolith, an Ayers Rock of the intellect, creativity, art and scientific advancement, but a laundry list which places the Romantics, Heidegger and Habermas in easy and apparently effortless apposition seems even less useful an idea with which to think about the Enlightenment. Mohandas Gandhi, an inveterate critic of Western civilization, found a West within the West with which he could work and with which he sought intellectual and political alliances; yet, as is obvious from his initiation of the idea of satyagraha, indeed from his very critique of Western modernity in *Hind Swaraj* (1909), he would also have looked askance at the idea that the West is the source of all our models of dissent. In the concluding chapter of *Inside Australian Culture*, our five authors attempt to move the discussion to another, equally important, register when they argue that Australian public culture has had an extraordinarily limited engagement with non-European cultural and intellectual traditions. The late J. V. D'Cruz described Australia's 'ambivalence towards Asia',[21] an ambivalence that may be gauged, as an example, from the fact that even as Australian politicians have, in keeping with trends elsewhere in the world, become more aware in recent years of China and declared an abiding interest in turning towards Asian countries as their natural and proximate partners, they have also agreed to a considerably enhanced American military presence as an open warning to China that Australia's Anglo heritage and 'old world' ties remain a constant in its foreign policy and intellectual outlook. President Obama's visit to Australia in November 2011, which culminated in an agreement that would station a full US marine task force of 2500 personnel on Australia's soil, is bound to send an unmistakable signal to Asian countries that Australia has no intent of abandoning its role as a junior enforcer of Pax Americana.

Far reaching as their critique is of Enlightenment Australia, our five authors might perhaps have gestured more forcefully at other models of interculturality and intellectual exchanges in their near vicinity. Indonesia is the closest landmass to Australia, barring Papua New Guinea, and the two countries enjoy a reasonably healthy economic trade with each other. Indonesia's political history over the last six decades, commencing with the mass purges against the communists in the 1950s and subsequently the stringent but eventually unsuccessful repression of secessionists from East Timor, may not be very inspiring to those inclined towards democratic sentiments, but there can be no doubt that the long history of Indonesia constitutes one of the more remarkable narratives of ecumenism and religious plurality. Though it has become commonplace to speak of Muslim terrorists, and to suppose that Islam is uniquely afflicted by the scourge of violent extremism, one would be hard pressed to find many countries that have long accommodated, in the fashion of Indonesia, the adherents of Hinduism, Buddhism, Islam, Protestantism and Catholicism, or that have lived with cultural and linguistic diversity with such ease. However, Australians have never looked to Indonesia as anything more than a playground and a sunny exotic retreat; had it been otherwise, they may have found in it a model of cultural pluralism and syncretic practices which would make the fabled narrative of the Enlightenment as a repository of values of tolerance, goodness and reason look extremely suspect. *Inside Australian Culture* is, nevertheless, a bold beginning in Australia's turn to other pasts and intellectual traditions as some of its citizens endeavour to produce a more just and equitable society for all of its peoples.

NOTES

Preface and Acknowledgements

1 Review comment by Raewyn Connell, *As Others See Us: The Australian Values Debate*, ed. J. V. D'Cruz, Bernie Neville, Devike Goonewardene and Phillip Darby (North Melbourne, Victoria: Australian Scholarly Publishing, 2008).

2 D'Cruz et. al, eds. *As Others See Us: The Australian Values Debate*.

3 Gloria Davies, J. V. D'Cruz and Nathan Hollier, eds, *Profiles in Courage: Political Actors and Ideas in Contemporary Asia* (North Melbourne, Victoria: Australian Scholarly Publishing, 2008).

4 Raewyn Connell, *Southern Theory: The Global Dynamics of Knowledge in Social Science* (Sydney: Allen and Unwin, 2007).

5 In his final year, starting in Chennai, India, and ending in Melbourne, Australia, D'Cruz penned a remarkable essay that was initially distributed at his funeral and later published. This essay lays out in the most comprehensive way the key concerns of his scholarship and life. See: J. V. D'Cruz, 'Little Cultures, Local Histories and National Literatures', *Reading Down Under: Australian Literary Studies Reader*, ed. Amit Sarwal and Reema Sarwal (New Delhi: SSS Publications, 2009).

6 J. V. D'Cruz and William Steele, *Australia's Ambivalence towards Asia* (Clayton, Melbourne: Monash Asia Institute, 2003).

7 Rosa Menocal, *The Ornament of the World: How Muslims, Jews, and Christians Created a Culture of Tolerance in Medieval Spain* (New York: Little, Brown, 2009).

Chapter One. Introduction

1 Edward Said, *Culture and Imperialism* (London: Vintage, 1984), 42.

2 Mick Dodson, 'Australia Day Needs to Encompass All of this Country's History', *Sydney Morning Herald* (27 January 2014): 14.

3 For an intelligent critique of Anzac, see Marilyn Lake and Henry Reynolds with Mark McKenna and Joy Damousi, *What's Wrong with Anzac: The Militarisation of Australian History* (Kensington, New South Wales: University of New South Press, 2010). This important scholarship, which continues to remain in the margins of mainstream thinking about Anzac, demonstrates the incapacity of Australia's public culture to adequately reflect on itself.

4 Ashis Nandy, *The Intimate Enemy* (New Delhi: Oxford University Press, 1981).

5 Interviewed in *The Beach*, Australian Broadcasting Corporation, 2001.

6 Quoted in Tony Hughes-d'Aeth, 'A Prospect of Future Regularity: Spatial Technologies in Colonial Australia', *Imagining Australian Space: Cultural Studies and Spatial Inquiry*, ed. Ruth Barcan and Ian Buchanan. (Perth: University of Western Australia Press, 1999), 47–58.

7 John Kane, 'Racialism and Democracy', *The Politics of Identity in Australia*, ed. Geoffrey Stokes (Cambridge: Cambridge University Press, 1997), 130.

8 Raewyn Connell, *Southern Theory: The Global Dynamics of Knowledge in Social Science* (Sydney: Allen and Unwin, 2007), 47.

9 Ien Ang and Jon Stratton, 'Asianising Australia: Notes towards a Critical Transnationalism in Cultural Studies', *Australia Cinema and Cultural Studies Reader*, ed. Amit Sarwal and Reema Sarwal (New Delhi: SSS Publications, 2009), 321.

10 For a more complete history of his scholarship, see J. V. D'Cruz, 'Little Cultures, Local Histories and National Literatures', *Reading Down Under: Australian Literary Studies Reader*, ed. Amit Sarwal and Reema Sarwal (New Delhi: SSS Publications, 2009).

11 Henry Reynolds, *This Whispering in Our Hearts* (St. Leonards, NSW: Allen and Unwin, 1998), 3.

12 John Gascoigne, *The Enlightenment and the Origins of European Australia* (Cambridge: Cambridge University Press, 2002).

13 Ang and Stratton, 'Asianising Australia', 231.

14 J. V. D'Cruz, 'Little Cultures, Local Histories and National Literatures', xxxvii.

15 In 2001, the Howard Government refused permission for MV Tampa, a Norwegian freighter carrying 438 mainly Afghani refugees, to enter Australian waters despite a humanitarian emergency.

16 See, for example, Samantha Maiden, 'PM Caught in Policy Bind', *Australian* (9 November 2009): 2; Mike Steketee, 'Held Hostage by the Rush to Be Tough', *Australian* (7 November 2009): 8; and Paul Kelly, 'Rudd's Softer Stance Mugged by Reality', *Australian* (17 October 2009): 11.

17 D'Cruz, 'Little Cultures, Local Histories and National Literatures', xxi.

18 David Walker, *Anxious Nation: Australia and the Rise of Asia, 1850–1939*, (St Lucia: Queensland University Press, 1999).

19 Baden Offord has argued elsewhere in support of Aboriginal scholar Aileen Moreton-Robinson's challenge to Australian society that there needs to be honest recognition and acceptance of Aboriginal ontological belonging. This is not to deny non-Indigenous belonging in Australia, which has its own story, but it is an important and critical step in Australia's reconciliation and decolonising process. See Baden Offord, 'Landscapes of Exile (and Narratives on the Trauma of Belonging)', *Landscapes of Exile: Once Perilous, Now Safe*, Anna Haebich and Baden Offord, eds., (London: Peter Lang, 2008), 1–9.

20 There are a number of recent excellent works extant that demonstrate robust intellectual orientations towards a reflective Australian culture from a range of non-Anglo-Celtic perspectives. See, for example, Suvendrini Perera, *Australia and the Insular Imagination: Beaches, Borders, Boats, and Bodies* (New York: Palgrave Macmillan, 2009); Olivia Khoo, Belinda Smaill and Audrey Yue, *Transnational Australian Cinema: Ethics in the Asian Diasporas* (Lexington, USA: Rowman & Littlefield, 2013); Alice Pung, *Growing Up Asian in Australia* (Melbourne: Black Inc., 2008); Regina Ganter, *Mixed Relations: Asian-Aboriginal Contact in North Australia* (Perth: University of Western Australia Press, 2006); Tseen Khoo (ed.), *Locating Asian Australian Cultures* (London: Routledge, 2008); Peta Stephenson, *The Outsider's Within: Telling Australia's Indigenous-Asian Story* (Kensington: UNSW Press, 2007); and Laksiri Jayasuriya, *Transforming a 'White Australia': Issues of Racism and Immigration* (New Delhi: SSS Publications, 2012).

21 Deborah Bird Rose, *Reports from a Wild Country: Ethics for Decolonisation* (Kensington, New South Wales: UNSW Press, 2004), 24.

22 Mick Dodson, 'Australia Day Needs to Encompass All of this Country's History', 14.

23 Soenke Biermann, 'Knowledge, Power and Decolonization', *Indigenous Philosophies and Critical Education*, ed. George Dei (New York: Peter Lang, 2011), 386–98, 394.

24 Ghassan Hage, *Against Paranoid Nationalism* (Annandale: Pluto Press, 2003), 94.

25 Andrew Robinson, 'In Theory Bakhtin: Dialogism, Polyphony and Heteroglossia', *Ceasefire*, http://ceasefiremagazine.co.uk/in-theory-bakhtin-1/, July 2011, accessed 20 November 2013.

26 David Malouf, *Remembering Babylon* (Milson's Point: Random House, 1993), 130.

Chapter Two. The Enlightenment and Tradition in Early Colonial Society

 1 John Gascoigne, *The Enlightenment and the Origins of European Australia* (Cambridge: Cambridge University Press, 2002), 9.

 2 There has been considerable scholarship dispelling the idea that there is a single project that can be termed 'the Enlightenment', and emphasising the diversity of Enlightenment ideas across different sociohistorical contexts. See, for example, John Pocock, *Barbarism and Religion, The Enlightenments of Edward Gibbon*, vol 1 (Cambridge: Cambridge University Press, 1999).

 3 See John Robertson, *The Case for the Enlightenment* (Cambridge: Cambridge University Press, 2005), 28–30.

 4 Gascoigne, *The Enlightenment and the Origins of European Australia*, 10.

 5 Alan Atkinson, *The Europeans in Australia* (Oxford: Oxford University Press, 1997), 106.

 6 Roy Porter, *Enlightenment: Britain and the Creation of the Modern World* (London: Penguin Books, 2000), 306.

 7 Henry Reynolds, *The Law of the Land* (Ringwood, Victoria: Penguin, 1992), 12–29; Kay Anderson, *Race and the Crisis of Humanism* (Milton Park: Routledge 2007), 44–8.

 8 A. T. Yarwood and M. J. Knowling, *Race Relations in Australia: A History* (Sydney: Methuen, 1983), 15–17.

 9 Gascoigne, *The Enlightenment and the Origins of European Australia*, 69–99.

10 Porter, *The Enlightenment: Britain and the Creation of the Modern World*, 15.

11 For example, Jeremy Bentham, 'A Pleas for the Constitution: Shewing the Enormities Committed to the Oppression of British Subjects, Innocent as Well as Guilty, in Breach of Magna Charta, the Petition of Right, the Habeas Corpus Act, and the Bill of Rights; as likewise of the Several Transportation Acts; in and by the Design, Foundation and Government of the Penal Colony of New South Wales', *The Works of Jeremy Bentham*, ed. John Bowring, vol. 4 (Edinburgh: William Tait, 1843). This pamphlet was not published in Bentham's lifetime, but a copy of it reached Sydney through David Collins. See Atkinson, *The Europeans in Australia*, 262–3.

12 Gascoigne, *The Enlightenment and the Origins of European Australia*, 42. See also A. Atkinson, 'Jeremy Bentham and the Rum Rebellion', *Journal of the Royal Australian Historical Society* 64, no. 1 (1978): 1–13.

13 Gascoigne, *The Enlightenment and the Origins of European Australia*, 38–49.

14 Atkinson, *The Europeans in Australia*, 6.

15 Robert Hughes, *The Fatal Shore* (London: Collins, 1987), 202.

16 Gascoigne, *The Enlightenment and the Origins of European Australia*, 103–115.

17 Gascoigne, *The Enlightenment and the Origins of European Australia*, 148–52; Anderson, *Race and the Crisis of Humanism*, 48–63.

18 Quoted in Atkinson, *The Europeans in Australia*, 149.
19 Gascoigne, *The Enlightenment and the Origins of European Australia*, 156.
20 David Theo Goldberg, 'Modernity, Race and Morality', *Race Critical Theories: Text and Context*, ed. Philomena Essed and David Theo Goldberg (Oxford: Blackwell, 2005), 296.
21 Donald Horne, *The Public Culture: The Triumph of Industrialism* (London: Pluto Press, 1986), 144.
22 Gascoigne, *The Enlightenment and the Origins of European Australia*, 19, 169.
23 Stephen Muecke, *Ancient and Modern: Time, Culture and Indigenous Philosophy* (Sydney: UNSW Press, 2004), 136.
24 Gascoigne, *The Enlightenment and the Origins of European Australia*, 71.
25 Robert Hughes, *This Fatal Shore*, 264–5, 265–6. Indeed, Bentham argued for a tolerant view of homosexuality and for its decriminalization. However, his views were not published in his lifetime. See Lea Campos Boralevi, *Bentham and the Oppressed* (New York: Walter de Gruyter, 1984), 37.
26 Robertson, *The Case for the Enlightenment*, 325. On the concern of the Enlightenment with progress rather than anticlericalism, see 8.
27 John Gray, *Liberalism* (Buckingham: Open University Press, 1995), 7.
28 Porter, *The Enlightenment: Britain and the Creation of the Modern World*, 99.
29 Gascoigne, *The Enlightenment and the Origins of European Australia*, 20.
30 Gray, *Liberalism*, 16–17
31 Gascoigne, *The Enlightenment and the Origins of European Australia*, 38.
32 Gascoigne, *The Enlightenment and the Origins of European Australia*, 114.
33 Robertson, *The Case for the Enlightenment*, 26.
34 Gray, *Liberalism*, 15–6.
35 Gascoigne, *The Enlightenment and the Origins of European Australia*, 39.
36 These British rights included rule of law, fair trial by one's peers, the right to life, freedom of movement and freedom of conscience and speech. See Alistair Davidson, *From Subject to Citizen: Australian Citizenship in the Twentieth Century* (Cambridge: Cambridge University Press, 1997), 143. This disjunction between liberalism and the Enlightenment is unique to England. Gray writes, 'Through out the latter half of the eighteenth century, the history of liberalism in continental Europe and the spread of the Enlightenment must be regarded as aspects of one and the same current of thought and practice. This was not so in England, where the victory of the parliamentary forces in the Glorious Revolution of 1688 inaugurated a long period of social and political stability in an individualist order under the aegis of the Whig nobility.' *Liberalism*, 17.
37 Davidson, *From Subject to Citizen*, 144.
38 Patrick Parkinson, *Tradition and Change in Australian Law* (Sydney: The Law Book Company, 1994), 3–14.
39 Gascoigne, *The Enlightenment and the Origins of European Australia*, 50.
40 Atkinson, *The Europeans in Australia*, 109.
41 Atkinson, *The Europeans in Australia*, 66.
42 W. K. Hancock, *Australia* (London: Jacaranda Press, 1930), 55.
43 David Beers Quinn, 'Sir Thomas Smith (1513–1577) and the Beginning of English Colonial Theory', *Proceedings from the American Philosophical Society* 85, no. 5 (1945): 543–60.
44 Of course, during the Enlightenment, the assertion that the non-European races lacked rationality and thus humanity was added to this arsenal. See Goldberg, 'Modernity, Race and Morality', 294.
45 Yarwood and Knowling, *Race Relations in Australia*, 18, 20.

46 Gascoigne, *The Enlightenment and the Origins of European Australia*, 21. See also 19–32.

47 Gascoigne, *The Enlightenment and the Origins of European Australia*, 111–16, 171.

48 Gascoigne, *The Enlightenment and the Origins of European Australia*, 145.

49 Anderson, *Race and the Crisis of Humanism*, 72, 77, 96; Gascoigne, *The Enlightenment and the Origins of European Australia*, 75.

50 Anderson, *Race and the Crisis of Humanism*, 87.

51 Tim Bonhady, *The Colonial Earth* (Melbourne: Melbourne University Press, 2000), 1–11.

52 Such an impact on Aboriginal Australians was profound. The Kombumerri intellectual and Elder, Aunty Mary Graham, has expressed it thus: 'One of the worst things that whitefellas did, when they came, wasn't the murders and the rapes, and the theft of land, bad as those things were […] the worst thing was that they brought this terrible idea with them that life was about survival […] about being a convict or a soldier and just making it from day to day, and they have infected our people with this awful idea.' Quoted in Melissa Lucashenko, 'Survival', *Pen Essays*, vol. 2, (Sydney: Allen and Unwin, 2009), 30.

53 Gascoigne, *The Enlightenment and the Origins of European Australia*, 157; Anderson, *Race and the Crisis of Humanism*, 100.

54 Quoted in Yarwood and Knowling, *Race Relations in Australia*, 12.

55 Yarwood and Knowling, *Race Relations in Australia*, 52.

56 See Henry Reynolds, *The Other Side of the Frontier* (Victoria: Penguin, 1990), 68–70 and Stephen Muecke, *Ancient and Modern*, 13–22.

57 Anderson, *Race and the Crisis of Humanism*, 97–100.

58 Reynolds, *The Other Side of the Frontier*.

59 Gascoigne, *The Enlightenment and the Origins of European Australia*, 158.

60 Gascoigne, *The Enlightenment and the Origins of European Australia*, 162.

61 Henry Reynolds, *This Whispering in Our Hearts* (St. Leonards, New South Wales: Allen and Unwin, 1998), 3.

62 Anderson, *Race and the Crisis of Humanism*, 109–189. See also Gascoigne, *The Enlightenment and the Origins of European Australia*, 164.

63 Gascoigne, *The Enlightenment and the Origins of European Australia*, 7.

64 Robertson, *The Case for the Enlightenment*, 42.

65 Goldberg, 'Modernity, Race and Morality', 297.

66 B. Semmel, 'The Philosophical Radicals and Colonialism', *Journal of Economic History* 21 (1961): 513–25.

67 Gascoigne, *The Enlightenment and the Origins of European Australia*, 76.

68 Roberston, *The Case for the Enlightenment*, 396.

69 Anderson, *Race and the Crisis of Humanism*, 190–203.

70 Muecke, *Ancient and Modern*, 9.

71 Lenore Coltheart and Peter Bridges, 'The Elephant's Bed? Scottish Enlightenment and the Foundations of New South Wales', *Journal of Australian Studies* 68 (2001): 19–34.

72 Gray, *Enlightenment's Wake* (Milton Park: Routledge, 1995), 64.

73 Dipesh Chakrabarty, *Provincializing Europe: Post-colonial Thought and Historical Difference* (Ewing, NJ: Princeton University Press, 2000), 7.

74 Ranajit Guha quoted in Chakrabarty, *Provincializing Europe*, 15.

75 The idea of a public culture is integrally part of Enlightenment political thinking. For those promulgating Enlightenment thought, the discussion of social and political matters needed to occur in public so that their independent authority could be heard. The notion of a public space in which people can freely discuss and critically debate public affairs is required for the challenging of traditional authority. Alistair Hannay,

On the Public (Milton Park: Routledge, 2005), 8–9. Robertson writes, 'the Enlightenment's conception of the progress of society was intimately connected to a novel view of how men of letters should seek influence over it, by appealing to public opinion rather than to rulers and their ministers.' *The Case for the Enlightenment*, 9.

Chapter Three. Australian Values and Their Public Culture(s)

1 Following Ghassan Hage, *Against Paranoid Nationalism* (Pluto Press: Sydney, 2003). The unfinished project of colonisation is not in itself continued by Britain, but by the installed colonial consciousness and its effects, which is manifest through the collective amnesia of its core institutions.
2 Danielle Wyatt, 'A Place in the Nation: Locality, Governmentality and Inhabiting the Waving Lands', *Journal of Australian Studies* 33, no. 4: 445–57, 446.
3 Quoted in Tim Wilson, 'Nothing Radical about Equal Opportunities for All Citizens', *The Australian*. 7 March 2007.
4 Donald Horne, *The Public Culture: An Argument with the Future* (Pluto Press: London, 1986).
5 Following an argument put forward by Craig Macgregor, *Sydney Morning Herald*, 23 October 1999.
6 Ien Ang, 'From White Australia to Fortress Australia: The Anxious Nation in the New Century', *Legacies of White Australia*, ed. Laksiri Jayasuriya, David Walker and Jan Gothard (Crawley, WA: University of Western Australia Press, 2003), 5.
7 Gloria Anzaldua, *Borderlands: The New Mestiza* (San Francisco: Spinsters/Aunt Lute Foundation, 1987), 3.
8 Janet Albrechtsen, 'Group Hugs Can Be Dangerous', *Australian*, 7 March 2007.
9 Janet Albrechsten, 'The Love We Dare Not Let Wed', *Australian*, 14 June 2006.
10 Janet Albrechsten, 'The Love We Dare Not Let Wed'.
11 John Howard, Address to the National Press Club Great Hall, Parliament House, http://www.pm.gov.au/media/speech/2006/speech1754.cfm, 2006, accessed 20 October 2013.
12 Wendy Brown, *Regulating Aversion: Tolerance in the Age of Identity and Empire* (Princeton, NJ: Princeton University Press, 2006).
13 Tony Thwaites, Lloyd Davis and Warwick Mules, *Tools for Cultural Studies: An Introduction* (South Melbourne: Macmillan, 1994), 208.
14 Ruth Lister, *Citizenship: Feminist Perspectives* (London: Macmillan, 1997), 3.
15 John Chesterman and Brian Galligan, eds, *Defining Australian Citizenship*. (Melbourne: Melbourne University Press, 1999), 1.
16 Department of Immigration, Multicultural and Indigenous Affairs, *What It Means to Be an Australian Citizen* (Canberra: Commonwealth Government, 1997; repr. 2002).
17 Madan Sarup, *Identity, Culture and the Postmodern World* (Edinburgh: Edinburgh University Press, 1996), 5.

Chapter Four. Moment One. An Act to Regulate Chinese Immigration (1858): Celestial Migrations

1 'Golden Horde' is best known as that part of the Mongol empire established in Russia in the thirteenth century. There are different explanations for the 'golden' colour including the steppe colour system of the cardinal directions.

2 Engel's letter to Marx on 23 September 1851, cited in Karen Fletcher, 'Why Celebrate Eureka?', *Green Left Online*, 1 December 2004, http://www.greenleft.org.au/2004/608/31259, accessed 10 October 2007.

3 Charles La Trobe, cited in Hamish Mcpherson, 'To Stand Truly by Each Other: The Eureka Rebellion and the Continuing Struggle for Democracy', http://www.anu.edu.au/polsci/marx/interventions/eureka.htm, accessed 8 October 2007.

4 Hamish Mcpherson, 'To Stand Truly by Each Other'.

5 Cited in M. Willard, *History of the White Australia Policy to 1920* (Carlton: Melbourne University Press, 1974), 21.

6 Eric Andrews, *Australia and China: The Ambiguous Relationship* (Carlton: Melbourne University Press, 1985), 8.

7 Sir H. Barkley, Sir C. Hotham, Despatches, no.118, 12 March 1957. Cited in Willard, *History*, 27.

8 J. V. D'Cruz, 'White Australia and the Indian Mutiny', *The Asia Image in Australia: Episodes in Australian History* (Melbourne: The Hawthorne Press, 1973), 11–31.

9 Charles Price, *The Great White Walls Are Built: Restrictive Immigration to North America and Australasia 1836–1888'* (Canberra: Australian National University Press, 1974), 76.

10 *Sydney Morning Herald*, 10 April 1858.

11 *Sydney Morning Herald*, 10 April 1858.

12 *Sydney Morning Herald*, 10 April 1858.

13 *Sydney Morning Herald*, 10 April 1858.

14 David Walker, 'Race Building and the Disciplining of White Australia', *Legacies of White Australia: Race Culture and Nation*, ed. Laksiri Jayasuriya, David Walker and Jan Gothard (Crawley, WA: University of Western Australia Press, 2003), 36.

15 *Sydney Morning Herald*, 10 April 1858.

16 *Sydney Morning Herald*, 10 April 1858.

17 *Sydney Morning Herald*, 10 April 1858.

18 *Sydney Morning Herald*, 21 July 1858.

19 *Sydney Morning Herald*, 21 July 1858.

20 *Sydney Morning Herald*, 21 July 1858.

21 *Sydney Morning Herald*, 22 July 1858.

22 *Sydney Morning Herald*, 22 July 1858.

23 *Sydney Morning Herald*, 22 July 1858.

24 Walker, 'Race Building', 43.

25 Walker, 'Race Building', 38.

26 Walker, 'Race Building', 38.

27 *Journal of the Legislative Council of NSW* 3 (1858): 331; 335; 389.

28 *Journal of the Legislative Council of NSW* 3 (1858): 321.

29 *Journal of the Legislative Council of NSW* 3 (1858): 321.

30 *Journal of the Legislative Council of NSW* 3 (1858): 321.

31 *Journal of the Legislative Council of NSW* 3 (1858): 321.

32 *Journal of the Legislative Council of NSW* 3 (1858): 321.

33 *Sydney Morning Herald*, 5 August 1858.

34 *Journal of the Legislative Council*, 27.

35 *Journal of the Legislative Council*, 27.

36 *Miner*, 6 March 1861, quoted in Ann Curthoys, 'Liberalism and Exclusionism', *Legacies of White Australia: Race Culture and Nation*, ed. Laksiri Jayasuriya, David Walker and Jan Gothard (Crawley, WA: University of Western Australia Press, 2003), 20.

37 *Miner*, 6 March 1861.

38 *Miner*, 6 March 1861.

39 Michel Foucault, *The History of Sexuality Volume 1* (Harmondsworth: Penguin, 1979), 38.

40 Foucault, *History of Sexuality Volume 1*, 42.

41 John Waller, *Discovery of the Germ* (Cambridge: Totem Books, 2002), 26, http://site. ebrary.com/lib/southerncross/Doc?id=10161006&ppg=35, accessed 6 October 2007.

42 Waller, *Discovery of the Germ*, 28.

43 *Journal of the Legislative Council*, 27.

44 D'Cruz, 'White Australia and the Indian Mutiny', 23.

45 *Journal of the Legislative Council*, 27.

46 *Journal of the Legislative Council*, 27.

47 *Journal of the Legislative Council*, 27.

48 *Journal of the Legislative Council*, 27.

49 *Journal of the Legislative Council*, 27.

50 *Journal of the Legislative Council*, 27.

51 D'Cruz, 'White Australia and the Indian Mutiny', 24.

52 *Journal of the Legislative* Council, 27.

53 Alison Bashford, *Imperial Hygiene: A Critical History of Colonialism, Nationalism and Public Health* (New York: Palgrave Macmillan, 2004), 16.

54 Bashford, *Imperial Hygiene*, 16.

55 Bashford, *Imperial Hygiene*, 14–38.

56 *Journal of the Legislative Council*, 27.

57 Bashford, *Imperial Hygiene*, 138.

58 Bashford, *Imperial Hygiene*, 139.

59 *Journal of the Legislative Council*, 27.

60 *Sydney Morning Herald*, 30 October 1858.

61 *Sydney Morning Herald*, 30 October 1858.

62 *Sydney Morning Herald*, 30 October 1858.

63 David Goldberg, *Racist Culture: Philosophy and the Politics of Meaning* (Cambridge, MA: Blackwell, 1993), 4.

64 Charles Pearson, 'National Life and Character: A Forecast', 50, cited in D. Gibb, *The Making of 'White Australia'* (West Melbourne: Victorian Historical Association, 1973), 26.

65 John Kane, 'Racialism and Democracy', *The Politics of Identity in Australia*, ed. Geoffrey Stokes (Cambridge: Cambridge University Press, 1997), 124.

Chapter Five. Moment Two. *Cubillo v. the Commonwealth* (2000): The 'History Defence' – Standards of the Time

1 Senator Herron, minister for Aboriginal and Torres Strait Islander affairs, *Bringing Them Home*, Government Initiatives, 16 December 1997.

2 Brennan, 'Kruger v. the Commonwealth of Australia' (1997), 190 CLR 1, par. 36.

3 See, for example, Jennifer Clark, 'Commonwealth Not Liable: Cubillo and Gunner v. Commonwealth', *Indigenous Law Bulletin* (2000) http://www.austlii.edu.au/au/journals/ILB/2000/14.html, accessed 1 October 2012; Pam O'Connor, 'History on Trial: Cubillo and Gunner v. the Commonwealth of Australia', *Alternative Law Journal* 26, no. 1 (February 2001): 27–31; Judith Bessant, 'Procedural Justice, Conflict

of Interest and the Stolen Generations' Case', *Australian Journal of Public Administration* 63, no. 1 (March 2004): 74–84; Trish Luker, 'Intention and Iterability in Cubillo v. Commonwealth', *Journal of Australian Studies* 84 (2005): 35–42; Alisoun Neville, 'Cubillo v. Commonwealth: Classifying Text and the Violence of Exclusion', *Macquarie Law Journal* (2005), http://www.austlii.org/au/journals/MqLJ/2005/3.html, accessed 1 October 2012; Alisoun Neville, 'Cubillo v. Commonwealth: Classifying Text and the Violence of Exclusion', *Macquarie Law Journal* 5 (2005): 31–55; Alisoun Neville, 'An Isolation Within: Cubillo v. Commonwealth and the Absence of Value' [forthcoming].

4 This passage was reproduced by Justice O'Loughlin in his explanation of the judgement in the case of Cubillo v. the Commonwealth. The original passage appears in Nulyarimma v. Thompson (1999) 165 ALR 621 at 638–9. Cited in Justice O'Loughlin, Cubillo v. Commonwealth, no. 2 (2000): 91 FCR 1.

5 See Roseanne Kennedy, 'Stolen Generations Testimony: Trauma, Historiography, and the Question of "Truth"', *Aboriginal History* 25 (200): 116–31; Peter Read, 'The Stolen Generations, the Historians and the Court Room', *Aboriginal History* 26 (2002): 51–61; Dan Meagher, 'Regulating History: Australian Racial Vilification Law and History Denial', *University of Queensland Law Journal* (2005): 499–532; Joseph Pugliese, 'The Stranger in our Midst: History's Forgotten Doubles', *As Others See Us: The Values Debate in Australia*, ed. J. V. D'Cruz, Phillip Darby, Bernie Neville, Devika Goonewardene and Phillip Darby (Melbourne: Australian Scholarly Publishing, 2008), 79–89.

6 E. H. Carr, *What is History?* (Harmondworth: Penguin, 1961), 9.

7 Consider, for example, the work of Adam Ferguson in his *Essay on the History of Civil Society*. Ferguson shared with some of the other members of the Scottish intellectual elite a stadial argument about progress, an understanding of history as societies advancing from barbarism to refinement and a conviction that Europe exemplified progress towards a refined civilisation. Available online at Project Gutenberg, http://www.gutenberg.org/etext/8646, 2005, accessed 1 October 2012.

8 (2000): 103 FCR 1, 28–9.

9 (2000): 103 FCR 1, 14.

10 (2000): 103 FCR 1, 170.

11 (2000): 103 FCR 1, 508.

12 (2000): 103 FCR 1, 1264.

13 (2000): 103 FCR 1, 454.

14 (2000): 103 FCR 1, 147.

15 (2000): 103 FCR 1, 1142.

16 (2000): 103 FCR 1, 1142.

17 (2000): 103 FCR 1, 343.

18 (2000): 103 FCR 1, 343, 597.

19 (2000): 103 FCR 1, 625.

20 (2000): 103 FCR 1, 558.

21 (2000): 103 FCR 1, 1141, 1267.

22 (2000): 103 FCR 1, 635.

23 (2000): 103 FCR 1, 588.

24 (2000): 103 FCR 1, 605.

25 (2000): 103 FCR 1, 1259.

26 (2000): 103 FCR 1, 666.

27 (2000): 103 FCR 1, 1256, 1244.

28 (2000): 103 FCR 1, 1259.

29 (2000): 103 FCR 1, 1259.
30 For a full discussion of this point, see Trish Luker, 'Intention and Iterability in Cubillo v. Commonwealth', *Journal of Australian Studies*, no. 84 (2005), 35–42.
31 Clark has argued that the nature of protection laws need to be understood within the full scope of controls, of which there has been little debate and which challenges their treatment as beneficial in intent. See Jennifer Clark, 'Cubillo v. Commonwealth Case Notes' *Melbourne University Law Review* 7 (2001), 2, http://www.austlii.edu.au/au/journals/MULP/201/7.html, accessed 1 October 2012.
32 Chris Cunneen and Julia Grix, 'The Limitations of Litigation in Stolen Generations Cases', AIATSIS Discussion Paper, no. 15 (Canberra: Australian Institute of Aboriginal and Torres Strait Islander Studies, 2004), 25.
33 (2000): 103 FCR 1, 794–801.
34 Submission from Mr Milliken, acting director of the Welfare Branch to the administrator of the Northern Territory in 1957 (2000), 103 FCR 1, 802.
35 (2000): 103 FCR 1, 798.
36 (2000): 103 FCR 1, 1073.
37 (2000): 103 FCR 1, 1085.
38 (2000): 103 FCR 1, 96.
39 Peter Read, 'The Stolen Generations, the Historian and the Court Room', *Aboriginal History* 26 (2002), 54–5.
40 Read, 'The Stolen Generations', 54.
41 Read, 'The Stolen Generations', 55.
42 (2000): 103 FCR 1, 174.
43 (2000): 103 FCR 1, 176.
44 (2000): 103 FCR 1, 155.
45 Jerold Auerbach, *Justice without Law* (New York: New York University Press, 1983).
46 (2000): 103 FCR 1, 241. The letter was intended for Edna Rockliff, the joint secretary of the Status of Women's Council of the Australian Association for the United Nations, dated 23 November 1951.
47 (2000): 103 FCR 1, 241.
48 (2000): 103 FCR 1, 244.
49 (2000): 103 FCR 1, 1572.
50 (2000): 103 FCR 1, 1574.
51 J. Clarke, 'Cubillo v. Commonwealth Case Note', 286.
52 (2000): 103 FCR 1, 455.
53 (2000): 103 FCR 1, 799.
54 Cunneen and Grix, 'Limitations of Litigation', 24.
55 See Alisoun Neville, 'Cubillo v. Commonwealth: Classifying Text and the Violence of Exclusion', *Macquarie Law Journal* 5 (2005): 31–55.
56 Bain Attwood has expressed scepticism about collective memory and has argued for a distinction between the Stolen Generations narrative and history. See Bain Attwood, 'A Matter for History', *Australian Financial Review* (15 December 2000): 1–7, and 'The Stolen Generations and Genocide: Robert Manne's "In Denial: The Stolen Generations and the Right"', *Aboriginal History* 25 (2001): 163–71. For a discussion about the implications of Attwood's argument, see Roseanne Kennedy, 'Stolen Generations Testimony: Trauma, Historiography, and the Question of "Truth"', *Aboriginal History* 25 (2001): 116–62.
57 (2000): 103 FCR 1, 477.
58 (2000): 103 FCR 1, 137.

59 In a more recent case, the Supreme Court of South Australia awarded Bruce Trevorrow damages for negligence, breach of duty of care and breach of fiduciary and statutory duties relating to his removal from his family and detention. Trevorrow v. State of South Australia, no. 5, SASC 285, 1 August 2007. In this case, the documentation of Bruce Trevorrow's early years was described by Justice Gray as extensive. The judge expressed similar concern about the effect of contemporary attitudes on the witnesses, experts and legal advisers on their recall of events that took place 40 to 50 years ago (11). However, extensive contemporaneous documentation relevant to events was tendered: this was largely departmental, and witnesses were able to speak to documents and the procedures and practices they described. The judge was satisfied that the documents were a reliable record of events (14).

60 Raymond Evans and Bill Thorpe discuss this issue in relation to debates about Australian history, 'Indigenocide and the Massacre of Aboriginal History', *Overland*, no. 163 (Winter 2001), 25.

61 On this subject, see Dan Meagher, 'Regulating History: Australian Racial Vilification Law and History Denial', *University of Queensland Law Journal* 24 (2005): 499–532.

62 (2000): 103 FCR 1, 81.

63 Cunneen and Grix, 'Limitations of Litigation', 24.

64 David Theo Goldberg, 'Modernity, Race and Morality', *Race Critical Theories: Text and Context*, ed. Philomena Essed and David Theo Goldberg (Oxford: Blackwell, 2005), 297.

65 Russell McGregor, 'Degrees of Fatalism: Discourses on Racial Extinction in Australia and New Zealand', *Collisions of Cultures and Identities: Settlers and Indigenous Peoples*, ed. Patricia Grimshaw and Russell McGregor (Melbourne: RMIT Press, 2007), 246.

66 McGregor, 'Degrees of Fatalism', 246.

67 Hugh Morgan's claim that Aboriginal culture could not survive European settlement because it was not as strong as European culture, and Tim Fischer's pronouncement that Aboriginal culture had failed to invent the wheel or nation, are examples of the extent to which teleological notions of history and progress and relations of power and authority are still endemic in current political issues. Hugh Morgan and Tim Fischer were making comments on the political debate over the High Court decision in Australia to recognise native title. Hugh Morgan, a mining executive, was making an address to the Victorian RSL on 29 June 1993. See the *Sydney Morning Herald*, 2 July 1993, 1. Tim Fischer was leader of the Australian National Party. His comments were reported in the *Sydney Morning Herald*, 21 June 1993, and discussed the following day in the same newspaper in 'Letters to the Editor', 12.

68 Russell McGregor, 'Representations of the "Half-caste" in the Australian Scientific Literature of the 1930s', *Journal of Australian Studies*, no. 36, March 1993, 51–64

69 John Howard suggests, for example, that reconciliation will not work if it 'puts a higher value on symbolic gestures and overblown promises, rather than the practical needs of Aboriginal and Torres Strait Islander people in areas like health, housing, education and employment.' This suggests that practical responses are not symbolic and that symbolic gestures do not have resonance. The distinction being made and the inability to perform both operations simultaneously reflects a longstanding concern in Australia to make a virtue of pragmatism. From an edited version of the Prime Minister's opening address to the Australian Reconciliation Conference, 'Optimistic PM outlines his vision for future', *Sydney Morning Herald*, 27 May 1997, 6.

70 John Howard, cited in James Woodford, 'PM's Apology Draws Protest', *Sydney Morning Herald*, 27 May 1997, 1.

71 Herron, cited in Tony Wright, 'Majority Wants Official Apology', *Sydney Morning Herald*, 27 May 1997, 6.

72 Maria Giannacopoulos, 'The Nomos of Apologia', *Griffith Law Review* 18, no. 2 (2009): 331–50.

73 Robert Manne, 'The History Wars', *The Monthly*, November 2009, http://www.themonthly.com.au/nation-reviewed-robert-manne-comment-history-wars-2119, accessed 28 February 2010.

74 The claim that *Mabo* (no. 2) shows the ability of Australian law to fundamentally challenge the colonial vision of Aboriginal society is undermined by the fact that Mabo effectively defined the act of state doctrine that enabled white British sovereignty to override the validity of Aboriginal claims to land. As Irene Watson writes, 'The doctrine of *terra nullius* was used to legally annihilate Aboriginal peoples and this position has not been altered post-*Mabo* (no. 2)', 'The Future is Our Past: We Once Were Sovereign and We Still Are', *Indigenous Law Bulletin* 8, no. 2 (2012): 12, http://search.informit.com.au.ezproxy.scu.edu.au/fullText;dn=20130100;res=AGISPT, accessed 1 October 2012.

Chapter Six. Moment Three. Australian Localism and the Cronulla Riot (2005): The 'Barbaric Law' of 'He Who Was There First'

1 *National Nine News* [video recording], 11 December 2005, TCN9, Sydney.

2 Les Kennedy, Damien Murphy, Malcolm Brown and Tim Colquhoun, 'Our Racist Shame', *Sydney Morning Herald*, 12 December 2005, 1, 4.

3 Anne Davies and Stephanie Peatling, 'Australians Racist? No Way, Says Howard', *Sydney Morning Herald*, 13 December 2005, 6.

4 Greg Noble, '"Where the Bloody Hell Are We?" Multicultural Manners in a World of Hyperdiversity', *Lines in the Sand*, ed. Greg Noble (Annandale: Federation Press, 2009), 1–22.

5 Jeannette Edwards and Marilyn Strathern, 'Including Our Own', *Cultures of Relatedness*, ed. Janet Carsten (Cambridge: Cambridge University Press, 2000), 149–66.

6 Richard Howitt, 'Scale as Relation: Musical Metaphors of Geographical Scale', *Area* 30 (1998): 49–58; Sallie Marston, John Paul Jones III and Keith Woodward, 'Human Geography without Scale', *Transactions of the Institute of British Geographers* NS 30 (2005): 416–32.

7 Rhys Jones and Carwyn Fowler, 'Placing and Scaling the Nation', *Environment and Planning D: Society and Space* 25 (2007): 332–54.

8 *Four Corners* [video recording], 'Riot and Revenge', 13 March 2006, Australian Broadcasting Corporation. http://www.abc.net.au/4corners/content/2006/s15909 53.htm, accessed 15 November 2013.

9 Neil McMahon, 'A Lesson in Beach Etiquette and Good Manners – Shire-Style', *Sydney Morning Herald* (December 2005): 7, 10–11.

10 Kennedy et. al, 'Our Racist Shame', 1.

11 'Sarah' quoted in *Four Corners*, 'Riot and Revenge.'

12 *The 7:30 Report* [video recording], 12 December 2005, Australian Broadcasting Corporation.

13 For these territorial texts, see David Singh, 'White Subjectivity and Racial Terror: Towards an Understanding of Racial Violence', *Critical Race and Whiteness Studies* 3, no. 1 (2007): 7, http://www.acrawsa.org.au/files/ejournalfiles/70DavidSingh.pdf, accessed 15 November 2013; Catriona Elder, *Being Australian: Narratives of National Identity* (Crows Nest: Allen and Unwin, 2007), 305, Figure 11.3; Damien Murphy, 'Thugs Ruled the Streets, and the Mob Sang Waltzing Matilda', *Sydney Morning Herald* (12 December 2005): 4–5, 5, photograph; Gary Ramage, 'Respect Locals or Piss Off!' [photograph], *Daily Telegraph*, 12 December 2005, 6.

14 Kennedy et. al, 'Our Racist Shame', 1; Murphy, 'Thugs Ruled the Streets', 4.

15 Suvendrini Perera, 'Race Terror, Sydney, December 2005', *Borderlands e-Journal* 5, no. 1 (2006): §49, http://www.borderlandsejournal.adelaide.edu.au/vol5no1_2006/perera_raceterror.htm, accessed 25 October 2007.

16 Suvendrini Perera, '"Aussie Luck": The Border Politics of Citizenship Post Cronulla Beach', *ACRAWSA e-Journal* 3, no. 1 (2007): 1, http://www.acrawsa.org.au/journal/issues.htm, accessed 15 November 2013.

17 Perera, '"Aussie luck"', 5; Sutherland Shire Environment Centre, 'Kurnell – Birthplace of Modern Australia', http://www.ssec.org.au/our_environment/our_bioregion/kurnell/history/index.htm, 2008, accessed 15 November 2013.

18 Aileen Moreton-Robinson and Fiona Nicholl, 'We Shall Fight Them on the Beaches: Protesting Cultures of White Possession', *Journal of Australian Studies* 89 (2007): 149–6.

19 Moreton-Robinson and Nicholl, 'We Shall Fight', 149.

20 Cook's landing at Kurnell exemplifies the Enlightenment spirit in particular: scientific observation, mapping, description, collection and cataloguing.

21 For recent analysis, see Rob Garbutt, *The Locals: Identity, Place and Belonging in Australia and Beyond* (Bern: Peter Lang, 2011).

22 Jeanette Edwards, *Born and Bred: Idioms of Kinship and New Reproductive Technologies in England* (Oxford: Oxford University Press, 2000), 84.

23 Greg Myers, '"Where Are You From?" Identifying place', *Journal of Sociolinguistics* 10, no. 3 (2006): 320–43, 325 [emphasis in original].

24 For an analysis of *nationalist* rhetoric from supporters and opponents of the Cronulla riot, see Ana-Maria Bliuc, Craig McGarty, Lisa Hartley and Daniela Muntele Hendres, 'Manipulating National Identity: The Strategic Use of Rhetoric by Supporters and Opponents of the "Cronulla riots" in Australia', *Ethnic and Racial Studies*, 35, no. 12 (2012): 2174–94.

25 The analysis here broadly follows Fairclough's methodology for a critical language study, described in Norman Fairclough, *Language and Power*, 2nd ed. (Harlow: Pearson Education, 2001).

26 On media representation of Muslim men in Australian media, see as examples: Kiran Grewal, 'The "Young Muslim Man" in Australian Public Discourse', *Transforming Cultures* 2, no. 1 (2007): 116–34; Ryan Al-Natour, 'Folk Devils and the Proposed Islamic School in Camden', *Continuum* 24, no. 4 (2010): 573–85. For a feminist analysis, see Judy Lattas, '"Bikini vs. Burqa" in Contemporary Australia: A Feminist Response to the Cronulla Riots', *Lines in the Sand*, ed. Greg Noble (Annandale: Federation Press, 2009), 200–17.

27 The plural noun form of local, *locals*, has been chosen as it makes database searching and tabulation straightforward. Searching on the singular form, *local*, will also include occurrences of the adjective *local*. Locals, then, is a simple search item for a quick but effective analysis.

28 Mark Todd, 'The Natives are Restless', *Sydney Morning Herald* (5 November 2005): 27.

29 See, for example, Richard Hinds, 'Venus Vanishes – and I Don't Care What You Think', *Sydney Morning Herald*, 17 January 2006, 1.

30 Craig, 'View from the Beach', *Daily Telegraph* (7 December 2005): 40.

31 David de Vere, 'Let's Unite to Fight this Shame on the Beaches', letter to the editor, *Daily Telegraph*, 7 December 2005, 40.

32 *Daily Telegraph*, 'Calls for Calm as Locals Plot Revenge', 8 December 2005, 1.

33 Steve Gee and Luke McIlveen, 'Not on Our Beach – Cronulla Police Vow to Defend Australian Way', *Daily Telegraph*, 9 December 2005, 1.

34 Luke McIlveen, 'A Beast Surfaces – Battle of the Beach', *Daily Telegraph*, 9 December 2005, 1.

35 Syd Mitchell, 'Vigilantes Are up in Arms when Police Hands Tied', letter to the editor, *Daily Telegraph*, 10 December 2005, 24.

36 Luke McIlveen, Kara Lawrence and Gary Brooker, 'A Line in the Sand', *Daily Telegraph*, 10 December 2005, 68.

37 Clif Evers writes evocatively of the cultural reproduction of local practices, a 'sensual economy', as he puts it. See Clifton Evers, 'Locals Only!', *Proceedings of the Everyday Multiculturalism Conference*, ed. Selvaraj Velayutham and Amanda Wise, http://www.crsi.mq.edu.au/publications/conference_proceedings/, 28–9, September 2006, accessed 15 November 2013.

38 Mikhail Bakhtin, *Rabelais and His World*, trans. Helene Iswolsky (Cambridge: The MIT Press, 1968), 10.

39 Julia Kristeva, *Desire in Language: A Semiotic Approach to Literature and Art*, ed. Leon Roudiez, trans. Thomas Gora and others (Oxford: Basil Blackwell, 1980; repr. 1984), 71 [emphasis in original].

40 Stuart Hall, 'For Allon White: Metaphors of Transformation', *Stuart Hall: Critical Dialogues in Cultural Studies*, ed. David Morley and Kuan-Hsing Chen (London: Routledge, 1996), 287–305, 292.

41 Rob Garbutt, 'The Locals: A Critical Survey of the Idea in Recent Australian Scholarly Writing', *Australian Folklore* 21 (2006): 172–92, 175–9.

42 Tom Griffiths, *Hunters and Collectors: The Antiquarian Imagination in Australia* (Melbourne: Cambridge University Press, 1996), 220–21.

43 John Spurway, 'The Growth of Family History in Australia', *The Push: A Journal of Early Australian Social History* 27 (1989): 53–12, 61, 103. Both quotations are cited in Griffiths, *Hunters and Collectors*, 224.

44 Griffiths, *Hunters and Collectors*, 224.

45 Luke McIlveen and Kara Lawrence, 'Alcohol and Hate Shatter Summer Idyll', *Daily Telegraph*, 12 December 2005, 2.

46 McIlveen and Lawrence, 'Alcohol and Hate.'

47 'Steeley' quoted in *Daily* Telegraph, 'Gangs Are the Problem, Cries Local', 12 December 2005, 5.

48 *Daily Telegraph*, 'Back from the Void of Mob Rule', 13 December 2005, 18.

49 Ian Gregor, 'The Beauty of Australia is a Fair Go for All People', letter to the editor, *Daily Telegraph*, 14 December 2005, 32.

50 *Daily Telegraph*, 'More Power to the Rule of Law', 14 December 2005, 30.

51 Patricia Loughlan, 'Learn to Respect Each Other', letter to the editor, *Daily Telegraph*, 14 December 2005, 32.

52 Warren Jack, 'Time to Re-examine Our Cultural Policy', letter to the editor, *Daily Telegraph*, 17 December 2005, 20.

53 Theodor Adorno, *Minima Moralia: Reflections from Damaged Life*, trans. E. F. N. Jephcott (London: Verso, 1978), 155.

54 Richard Davis, 'Introduction: Transforming the Frontier in Contemporary Australia', *Dislocating the Frontier: Essaying the Mystique of the Outback*, ed. Deborah Bird Rose and Richard Davis (Canberra: ANU e-Press, 2005), 7–22, 8.

55 Rob Garbutt, 'White "Autochthony"', *Critical Race and Whiteness Studies* 2, no. 1 (2006): http://www.acrawsa.org.au/files/ejournalfiles/88RobGarbutt.pdf, accessed 15 November 2013.

56 Rob Garbutt, 'Local Order', *M/C Journal* 7, no. 6 (2005): §III, http://journal.media-culture.org.au/, accessed 15 November 2013.

57 John Chesterman and Brian Galligan, *Citizens without Rights: Aborigines and Australian Citizenship* (Melbourne: Cambridge University Press, 1997), 87–8; Anthony Trollope, *Australia*, ed. P. D. Edwards and R. B. Joyce (St Lucia: University of Queensland Press, 1967 [1873]), 101.

58 Pal Ahluwalia, 'When Does a Settler Become a Native? Citizenship and Identity in a Settler Society', *Pretexts: literary and cultural studies* 10, no. 1 (2001): 63–73, 64–5.

59 Mahmood Mamdani, 'When Does a Settler Become a Native? The Colonial Roots of Citizenship', *Pretexts: Studies in Writing and Culture* 7, no. 2 (1998): 249–58, 251; Ahluwalia 'When Does a Settler Become a Native', 66.

60 Griffiths, *Hunters and Collectors*, 220, 224.

61 Edwards, *Born and Bred*, 84.

62 Edwards, *Born and Bred*, 28.

63 Edwards, *Born and Bred*, 84.

64 McIlveen and Lawrence, 'Alcohol and Hate'; *Four Corners*, 'Riot and Revenge'.

65 *National Nine News* [my emphasis]; Ramage, 'Respect Locals or Piss Off!'

66 Nigel Rapport, 'The Morality of Locality: On the Absolutism of Landownership in an English Village', *The Ethnography of Moralities*, ed. Signe Howell (London: Routledge, 1997) 74–97, 74–5.

67 Edwards and Strathern, 'Including Our Own', 149.

68 Edwards and Strathern, 'Including Our Own', 153.

69 Kay Anderson, *Race and the Crisis of Humanism* (London: Routledge, 2007), 44–6.

70 Anderson, *Race and the Crisis of Humanism*, 44.

71 John Locke, *Two Treatises of Government*, ed. Peter Laslett (Cambridge: Cambridge University Press, 1988/1698): II§32 and II§45 [emphases in original].

72 On first possession, see Cheryl Harris, 'Whiteness as Property', *Harvard Law Review* 166 (1993): 1708–91, 1726–7, especially n. 68.

73 Peter Read, *Belonging: Australians, Place and Aboriginal Ownership* (Oakleigh: Cambridge University Press, 2000), 117.

Chapter Seven. The Closing of Public Culture to Communal Difference

1 J. V. D'Cruz, 'Little Cultures, Local Histories and National Literatures', *Reading Down Under: Australian Literary Studies Reader*, ed. Amit Sarwal and Reema Sarwal (New Delhi: SSS Publications, 2009), xxxiii.

2 Stephen Muecke, 'Cultural Studies in an Old Country', *Australia Cinema and Cultural Studies Reader*, ed. Amit Sarwal and Reema Sarwal (New Delhi: SSS Publications, 2009), 551.

3 Vijay Mishra and Robert Hodge, 'What is Post(-)Colonialism?', *Australian Cultural Studies: A Reader*, ed. John Frow and Meaghan Morris (St Leonards: Allen and Unwin, 1993), 39.

4 Ashis Nandy, 'Introduction: Science as Reason of State', *Science, Hegemony and Violence*, ed. Ashis Nandy (Bombay: Oxford University Press, 1988), 11.

5 Raewyn Connell, *Southern Theory: The Global Dynamics of Knowledge in Social Science* (Sydney: Allen and Unwin, 2007), 183–7.

6 Ashis Nandy, 'Australia's Polyglot Ghosts and Tireless Ghostbusters: A Demonic Foreword', *As Others See Us*, ed. J. V. D'Cruz, Bernie Neville, Devika Goonewardene and Phillip Darby (Melbourne: Australian Scholarly Publishing, 2008), xi–xxiv.

7 *Sydney Morning Herald*, 21 July 1858.

8 *Sydney Morning Herald*, 21 July 1858.

9 Nandy writes, 'However, much of the post-colonial world has borrowed its political categories not from living political realities in the West, but from Western texts and ideas that were exported to the tropics during the heyday of colonialism. The politics that contextualised the translation of texts and ideas into political practice and everyday culture of politics in the West, moderating the purism of formal political thought and scholarly convictions, never really fascinated the modern intelligentsia and public figures in the South.' Ashis Nandy, 'Coping with the Politics of Faiths and Cultures', *Time Warps: The Insistent Politics of Silent and Evasive Pasts* (Delhi: Permanent Black, 2001), 95.

10 Nandy writes that 'the traditional ways of life have, over the centuries, developed internal principals of tolerance, and that these principles must have play in contemporary politics.' 'The Politics of Secularism and the Recovery of Religious Tolerance', *Time Warps: The Insistent Politics of Silent and Evasive Pasts* (Delhi: Permanent Black, 2001), 79.

11 Ashis Nandy, 'Time Travel to a Possible Self: Searching for the Alternative Cosmopolitanism of Cochin', *Time Warps: The Insistent Politics of Silent and Evasive Pasts* (Delhi: Permanent Black, 2001), 206.

12 For a discussion of what such a tolerance between multicultural groups might look like, see Erika Kerruish, Baden Offord and J. V. D'Cruz, 'Teaching Shared Values and Social Cohesion: The Necessary Other', *As Others See Us*, ed. J. V. D'Cruz, Bernie Neville, Devika Goonewardene and Phillip Darby (Melbourne: Australian Scholarly Publishing, 2008), 103–7.

13 There is, Nandy demonstrates, a 'linkage in the popular culture of modernity between the ideology of adulthood and masculinity, on the one hand, and the ideology of modern science and technology, on the other', 141. Ashis Nandy, 'From Outside the Imperium: Gandhi's Cultural Critique of the West', *Traditions, Tyranny and Utopias* (Oxford: Oxford University Press, 1987), 143.

14 Nandy, 'From Outside the Imperium: Gandhi's Cultural Critique of the West', 141.

15 Ashis Nandy, 'The Traditions of Technology', *Traditions, Tyranny and Utopias* (Oxford: Oxford University Press, 1987), 87.

16 Ashis Nandy, 'Culture, Voice and Development: A Primer for the Unsuspecting', *The Romance of the State* (New Delhi: Oxford University Press, 2002), 159.

17 Nandy, 'From Outside the Imperium', 142.

18 Ashis Nandy, 'Science, Authoritarianism and Culture', *Traditions, Tyranny and Utopias* (Oxford: Oxford University Press, 1987), 116. Science and technology becomes a means to exclude that which is potentially acceptable within a democratic framework. But the arguments for the exclusion of the Chinese from the state of NSW, based on reasons of hygiene and sexuality, remained within the democratic institution of the

parliamentary inquiry. Fortunately, with the rejection of the bill, the point at which 'the invitation which the culture of modern science extends to state power to use scientific knowledge outside the reaches of the democratic process' was not reached. Nandy, 'Introduction: Science as Reason of State', 2.

19 J. V. D'Cruz, 'White Australia and the Indian Mutiny', *The Asian Image in Australia: Episodes in Australian History* (Melbourne: The Hawthorne Press, 1973), 26.
20 D'Cruz, 'White Australia and the Indian Mutiny', 30.
21 See Trish Lukar for a discussion of this reduction of history to law. *The Rhetoric of Reconciliation: Evidence and Judical Subjectivity in Cubillo v. Commonwealth 2000*, PhD Dissertation (Victoria: Latrobe University, 2006), 155–71.
22 Ashis Nandy, 'History's Forgotten Doubles', *History and Theory* 34, no. 2 (May 1995), 61.
23 Nandy, 'History's Forgotten Doubles', 50.
24 Nandy, 'History's Forgotten Doubles', 44.
25 Nandy, 'Coping with the Politics of Faiths and Cultures', 103–4.
26 James (Sákéj) Youngblood Henderson, 'Postcolonial Indigenous Legal Consciousness', *Indigenous Law Journal* 1 (Spring 2002): 1–56.
27 Nandy, 'Culture, Voice and Development: A Primer for the Unsuspecting', 156.
28 Ashis Nandy, 'Shamans, Savages and the Wilderness: On the Audibility of Dissent and the Future of Civilizations', *Bonfire of Creeds* (New Delhi: Oxford University Press, 2004), 477.
29 Ashis Nandy, 'State, History and Exile in South Asian Politics: Modernity and the Landscape of Clandestine and Incommunicable Selves', *The Romance of the State* (New Delhi: Oxford University Press, 2002), 130.
30 Ziauddin Sardar, 'The A B C D (and E) of Ashis Nandy', *Dissenting Knowledges, Open Futures: The Multiple Selves and Strange Destinations of Ashis Nandy*, ed. Vinay Lal (New Delhi: Oxford, 2000), 220. For a discussion by Nandy, see 'Evaluating Utopias', *Traditions, Tyranny and Utopias* (Oxford: Oxford University Press, 1987), 1–19.
31 Justice O'Loughlin, 'Cubillo v. Commonwealth', no. 2 (2000): 91 FCR 1, [1562].
32 Nandy, 'Evaluating Utopias', 7.
33 Scott Poynting, Greg Noble, Paul Tabar and Jock Collins, *Bin Laden in the Suburbs* (Sydney: Sydney Institute of Criminology Series, 2004), 12.
34 Since Fiske, Hodge and Turner's chapter on the beach in *Myths of Oz*, the beach has been a focus for Australian cultural studies' examination of national identity (Sydney: Allen and Unwin, 1987).
35 Baden Offord, 'Surfing Towards Australian Androgyny: Aussie Bums on the Beach', *As Others See Us*, ed. J. V. D'Cruz et al. (Melbourne: Australian Scholarly Press, 2008), 149–64.
36 Amelia Johns, 'White Tribe: Echoes of the Anzac Myth in Cronulla', *Continuum* 22, no. 1 (2008): 11.
37 Katherine Bode, 'Aussie Battler in Crisis? Shifting Cultural Constructions of White Australian Masculinity and National Identity?', 343.
38 Amelia Johns, 'White Tribe: Echoes of the Anzac Myth in Cronulla', 14.
39 Nandy, 'State, History and Exile in South Asian Politics: Modernity and the Landscape of Clandestine and Incommunicable Selves', 119–23.
40 Nandy, 'History's Forgotten Doubles', 55–6.
41 Ashis Nandy, 'Twilight of the Certitudes: Secularism, Hindu Nationalism and Other Masks of Deculturation', *Romance of the State* (New Delhi: Oxford University Press, 2002), 79–82.

42 Ghassan Hage, *Against Paranoid Nationalism* (London: Merlin Press, 2003), 55.

43 Nandy, 'Culture, Voice and Development', 156.

44 Nandy, 'Evaluating Utopias', 13.

45 Nandy, 'Science, Authoritarianism and Culture', 120.

46 Regarding the possibility for genuine dialogue between cultures, Nandy writes that 'according to the dominant format, a dialogue between two visions is established when one of them is seen as the framework, tool or theory for understanding the other, serving as the object of interpretation and as a reservoir of implicit or latent insights which could be useful or enriching for the former. […] One must, however, be aware that this approach often draws upon the arrogance of the modern world and ethnocentricism towards non-modern cultures and past time. The approach assumes that if one examines an ancient, marginalised vision in terms of a modern one and shows the former to be radical, scientific or rational, one has established a dialogue between the two.' Nandy, 'Evaluating Utopias', 15.

47 Nandy, 'Time Travel to a Possible Self: Searching for the Alternative Cosmopolitanism of Cochin', 206.

48 Nandy, *Talking India*, 57.

49 Nandy, 'Time Travel to a Possible Self: Searching for the Alternative Cosmopolitanism of Cochin', 206.

50 D'Cruz, 'Little Cultures, Local Histories and National Literatures', xxv–xxvi.

51 Ashis Nandy, 'The State: The Fate of a Concept', *The Romance of the State* (New Delhi: Oxford University Press, 2002), 2.

Afterword. The Emptiness Within and Without:
Enlightenment Australia and Its Demons

1 M. K. Gandhi, *An Autobiography or The Story of My Experiments with Truth*, trans. Mahadev Desai (Ahmedabad: Navajivan Publishing House, 1959 [1927]), 221.

2 Ernest Renan, 'What Is a Nation?', original French title, 'Qu'est-ce qu'une nation?' (1882), http://www.nationalismproject.org/what/renan.htm, accessed 15 April 2012.

3 Roland Barthes, *Empire of Signs*, trans. Richard Howard (New York: Hill and Wang, 1993).

4 Larry Wolff, *Inventing Eastern Europe: The Map of Civilization on the Mind of the Enlightenment* (Stanford: Stanford University Press, 1996).

5 Most readers would have surmised the presence of Walter Benjamin in my formulation: 'There is no document of civilization which is not at the same time a document of barbarism.' See his 'Theses on the Philosophy of History', *Illuminations*, trans. Harry Zohn and ed. Hannah Arendt (New York: Schocken, 1969), 256. However, I came to Benjamin long after reading Gandhi, whose *Hind Swaraj or Indian Home Rule* (Ahmedabad: Navajivan Publishing House, 1909) strikes me, however odd it may seem to sophisticated readers in the academy, as anticipating Benjamin in many respects. Chapter VI of his manifesto is called 'Civilization', and Gandhi is gentle but unsparing in his characteristically homely way to bring home some bitter truths: 'Formerly, when people wanted to fight with one another, they measured between them their bodily strength; now it is possible to take away thousands of lives by one man working behind a gun from a hill. This is civilization.' The 'thousands of lives' Gandhi speaks of are those of colonized peoples; the lopsided encounters between Europeans and the natives of Asia, Africa and Australia have been recounted in many works, and the role of the

machine gun, which Gandhi would have seen in action during the Zulu Rebellion, in the unfolding of this narrative is insightfully etched in John Ellis, *Social History of the Machine Gun* (Baltimore: Johns Hopkins University Press, 1986). The modern equivalent of this invention, we may say, is the drone – the use of which, under the Nobel Peace Laureate Barack Obama, has intensified sharply. Much like the machine gun in its early years, the drone has been deployed largely against tribesmen and other 'primitives'; more interestingly, it is touted, if we can entertain the thought, as a document of civilization, since its proponents highlight the supposed fact that the drone is used only for targeted assassinations, generally spares the lives of the innocents and is intended to induce submission without the carpet bombing to which some states at war have been subjected since air power began to be widely used in the beginning of the twentieth century. Drones take to new heights the principle that has become increasingly enshrined as one of the key features of war in the postindustrial cybernetic age, namely the notion that soldiers or assassins – increasingly indistinguishable in our age – should themselves never be at any risk, and should be distanced from the theatre of war.

6 Cited by David Day, *Claiming a Continent: A New History of Australia*, 3rd ed. (Sydney: HarperCollins Publishers, 2001), 141.

7 Day, *Claiming a Continent*, 142.

8 Cited in Day, *Claiming a Continent*, 188.

9 Besides the references in *Inside Australian Culture*, there is A. Dirk Moses, ed., *Genocide and Settler Society: Frontier Violence and Stolen Indigenous Children in Australian History* (New York: Berghahn Books, 2004).

10 Warwick Anderson, *The Cultivation of Whiteness: Science, Health and Racial Destiny in Australia* (New York: Basic Books, 2003).

11 See Philip Clarke, *Where the Ancestors Walked: Australia as an Aboriginal Landscape* (Crows Nest, New South Wales: Allen & Unwin, 2003).

12 On Aboriginal systems of classification, see Peter Worsley, *Knowledges: Culture, Counterculture, Subculture* (New York: The New Press, 1997), 17–124.

13 The dream of man's complete conquest over nature lives on, notwithstanding all the pious pronouncements over the last few decades about the sanctity of mother Earth, even among those who are represented as the more enlightened among public figures in Europe and the West. There is more than a touch of hubris in Barack Obama's confident assertion, in his presidential inaugural address, that 'we will harness the sun and the winds and the soil to fuel our cars and run our factories' – a sentiment deeply steeped in a mechanical view of the universe.

14 The 2002 Australian film, *The Tracker* (starring David Gulpilil in the title role, and directed by Rolf de Heer), is a subtle, indeed gripping, exploration of the immensely mixed reactions engendered by the Aboriginal tracker, who is simultaneously ridiculed, loathed, feared and envied, grudgingly acknowledged and yet cast as suspiciously human. Three white men – the fanatic, the follower and the veteran – in pursuit of an Aboriginal accused of murdering a white woman take the help of an Aboriginal tracker (Gulpilil). When the trail appears all but lost to the white men, the tracker finds the way. There are many parables here, as the torchbearers of 'civilization' are reduced to becoming followers; the fanatic, a specimen of rank racism, finally shackles the tracker and compels him to carry chains. Nothing in European epistemology had prepared the white man to accept the idea that there could be forms of knowledge that might be impermeable to his canons of reasoning or insight: though the shackles are placed around the tracker's neck, it is the white man who was stupendously hobbled by the weight of his own knowledge.

15 Stephen Greenblatt, *Marvelous Possessions: The Wonder of the New World* (Chicago: University of Chicago Press, 1991).

16 The classic work here is Paul Carter, *The Road to Botany Bay: An Exploration of Landscape and History* (Chicago: The University of Chicago Press, 1987).

17 Theodor Adorno, *Minima Moralia: Reflections from Damaged Life*, trans. E. F. N. Jephcott (London: Verso, 1978), 155.

18 Sankar Muthu, *Enlightenment against Empire* (Princeton, New Jersey: Princeton UP, 2003).

19 Lydia Liu, 'Translingual Practice: The Discourse of Individualism between China and the West', *Positions: East Asia Cultural Critiques* 1, no. 1 (Spring 1993), 191.

20 Dipesh Chakrabarty, *Habitations of Modernity: Essays in the Wake of Subaltern Studies* (Chicago: University of Chicago Press), 25.

21 J. V. D'Cruz and William Steele, *Australia's Ambivalence towards Asia: Politics, Neo/Post-colonialism, and Fact/Fiction*, rev. ed. (Clayton: Monash Asia institute, 2003).

INDEX

Muslim Australians 39
Muslims xiv, 79

Nandy, Ashis vii–xv, 2–5, 10–11,
    15, 33, 47, 63, 79, 97–113
narratives of belonging 10
Native Affairs Branch 74
Nelson, Lorna Napanangka 68
New Norcia 27
Nicholl, Fiona 82
non-British traditions 3, 108

Offord, Baden 109
O'Loughlin, Justice Maurice 68–73,
    75, 108
Orientalist 119
Ottoman Empire 58

Pacific Islander 48
Paine, Thomas 19
Parkes, Henry 50, 117
Parkinson, Patrick 24
Pearson, Charles 60
Perera, Suvendrini 82
political psychology 3
Porter, Roy 18
postcolonial studies xv
Price, Charles 49
public culture x, 34, 97
public sphere xiv, 18, 32–8, 40–43, 80,
    83, 97, 111–12

race 85
race-specific laws 76
racial identity 4
racial violence 86
racial-purity policies 72
racism 7, 43, 76–7, 87, 115
Read, Peter 72, 93, 104
Reconciliation Convention (1997) 77
Reeta Dixon Home 68
religion 20, 23, 26, 35, 63, 91,
    100, 119
Reynolds, Henry 6, 27–8
Reynolds, John 27
rights discourse 18, 28–9
Robb, Andrew 38
Robertson, John 16

Rose, Deborah Bird 9
Rudd Government 77
Rudd, Kevin 40
Rum Rebellion 18
Ruskin, John viii

Said, Edward 1
Sardar, Ziauddin 107
scientific knowledge 17
Scottish Enlightenment 17
Sculthorpe, Peter 3
self-definition ix–x, 1–2, 8, 10, 36–8,
    43, 91, 113
self-definition, Australia's x, 10
settler localism 80
settler society 1–2, 16
site hardening 34
Smith, Adam 17
Snow, C. P. vii
social cohesion 40
social contract theories 20
social Darwinism 76
Southern theory 5
space 118
Stolen Generation 63–4, 75
Strathern, Marilyn 91
Surap, Medan 43

Tagore, Rabindranath viii
terra nullius 5, 90, 92
Third Reich viii
Thompson, James 60
tolerance 39, 100, 121
Tolstoy, Leo viii, 115
tradition 8, 112

un-Australian 85
Union Jack 87, 117
United States ix
universal principles 16

vaccination 58–9
values vii–xiii, 1–4, 8–10, 15, 21–2,
    25–8, 32–43, 47, 65–6, 72–3,
    78–80, 87, 93, 98–103,
    106–11
Victorian goldfields 48–9
Voltaire 116

www.ingramcontent.com/pod-product-compliance
Lightning Source LLC
Chambersburg PA
CBHW020003290326
41935CB00007B/282